Geneen Roth, who has been both fat and anorexic herself, lives and works in Santa Cruz, California. Since the publication of *Feeding the Hungry Heart* (also available in paperback from Grafton Books), she has been invited all over the United States to conduct her Breaking Free workshops for compulsive eaters.

By the same author

Feeding the Hungry Heart

GENEEN ROTH

Breaking Free
from Compulsive Eating

GRAFTON BOOKS

A Division of the Collins Publishing Group

LONDON GLASGOW
TORONTO SYDNEY AUCKLAND

Grafton Books
A Division of the Collins Publishing Group
8 Grafton Street, London W1X 3LA

A Grafton UK Paperback Original 1986

ISBN 0-586-06691-8

Printed and bound in Great Britain by
Collins, Glasgow

Set in Century Schoolbook and Helvetica

To my mother, Ruth Wiggs
To my father, Bernard Roth

For their grace, humour and willingness
to participate in the struggle
of loving and letting go.

Thank you.

Contents

Acknowledgements

Every year I watch the Academy Awards, and every year at least one recipient drones on and on about his mother, who held his hands before he played Peter Pan in fifth grade, and his girlfriend Laurie, and his aunt Tessie, and his friend Raymond, without all of whom he wouldn't be standing here tonight. Every year I think, For God's sake, get on with it.

This year, I realized that we never accomplish anything alone. This year, I learned that my passion to write and my perseverance to sit through hours when words are stuck in concrete three miles away is about half of what it takes to write a book. The other half is the encouragement, sustenance, and loving welcome I receive from the people in my life.

Sara Friedlander gave me daily, and when it was needed, hourly perspective, faith, anchoring, and glue. By her tolerance for dissonance, generosity with her feelings, and ability to work at relationships, she has taught me not to leave love when it gets hard. I thank Agatha Coffey for her willingness to do whatever the need of the moment demands and for lighting up my world in the process. For his friendship, which continues to be a living matrix of all the qualities to which I aspire, I thank Lew Fein. For his unending patience, suggestions and availability at any hour of the day or night, I thank David Avadon. For teaching me to trust what I know, seen and unseen, I thank Sally Blumenthal, my everyday friend. For pulling like a kite back to earth and kitchen and hearth, I thank Estelle Fein. For her wise editorial advice, grounding, and commitment to our ever-deepening friendship, I thank Babs Bohn. For his reassurance and support throughout the year, I thank Bruce Bratton. For her enthusiastic and thoughtful reading of my manuscript, I thank Debby Burgard. For his interest and steady background support, I thank Cliff Friedlander. For renewing me by providing a place where words could fall away, I thank Linda Maldonado-Barman, Maria Ramirez, Rachel Lundquist, Ken Baker, and Christopher Smith. For inspiring me to honour the creative process by her own example, I thank Georgia Kelly. For receiving me and making a home for all my roles, I thank my parents, my brother, Howard Roth, and my stepfather, Richard Wiggs. And for stirring the memory of a dream by his combination of reticence at being met and stark insistence to meet, I thank my muse, Ralph.

For gifts that have heightened the quality of my life and my writing on a less personal but far-reaching basis, I thank Alexandra Kennedy for the foundation she helped to build; Joseph Goldstein, Jack Kornfield, and Alan Clements, whose words continue to awaken me; Harry and Susan Ungar for providing a place to begin my Breaking Free workshops; Karl Marhenke for my typewriter and the belief it embodied; Ellen Bass, Louise Thornton, Florinda Colavin, and Lucy Diggs for encouraging me at the beginning; the participants in the Breaking Free workshops for teaching me about courage and vulnerability and change; and the twenty-two women from around the country who contributed to *Feeding the Hungry Heart* and were never given the appreciation or recognition that their commanding part in the book deserved. Finally, for the birth of my second book child, I thank my editor, Peg Parkinson, for the seed that only a parent can provide.

Introduction

In my previous book, *Feeding the Hungry Heart*, I described the humiliation of being called 'P.F.C' by boys in my high school. When the page proofs of the book arrived, I crossed out the story, then added it, then deleted it, then added it again. Although I believed that the telling of it would be helpful, the thought of revealing a secret I have never told anyone terrified me. I worried that people were going to make fun of me the way the boys in high school had. I worried that *they* were going to call me Pregnant Faced Cow. I was afraid in the way that the people I see in workshops are afraid: that if I told anyone the depths of my hell, they would use it against me, call me crazy.

Instead, readers called and they wrote to share their stories, their secrets. I was gratified and moved by the response to *Feeding the Hungry Heart*; it taught me that in the expression of what is raw and vulnerable, a healing can take place in the rawness and vulnerability of others. Still, the letters and phone calls were asking for more. One person wrote: 'I stayed up all night to finish your book. I feel like you understand me. But I don't know what to do now. Can you help?' Another wrote 'Please, Ms Roth . . . *Feeding the Hungry Heart* is only a beginning. You let your readers feel understanding and acceptance for themselves, you gave us hope, but you left us without any way to implement it. We need another book.'

I hadn't considered writing another book about compulsive eating; I wasn't sure I *wanted* to write another book about eating; I didn't know that I had anything further to say. But as the need became clear, the book asked to be written.

Breaking Free from Compulsive Eating gathers all I've learned in the past ten years – in therapy, relationships, workshops I've attended and led, retreats I've participated in, lectures I've given, letters and phone calls I've received. The book is a compilation of years of learning and struggling and loving funneled into and adapted for the purpose of resolving the conflicts at the root of compulsive eating. Because the process of breaking free is a very personal one – we all wrestle with different inner demons, though they manifest themselves in similar patterns of eating – this book is a very personal one. It is a travelogue of sights, feelings, and situations that my clients and I passed as we attempted to come to peace with the anxiety-fraught relationship between ourselves and our bodies, ourselves and food. *Breaking Free from Compulsive Eating* is a guide book to be used for daily support, direction, and encouragement. By providing tools to work with, and on which you can elaborate, it translates the gentle philosophy of the Breaking Free workshops – trusting yourself, nourishing yourself, accepting yourself – into daily actions and beliefs.

Although I have inferred throughout the book that a major factor in being fat is compulsive eating, I want to stress that I do not believe that all people who are overweight are compulsive eaters. Despite the voluminous amount of research on dieting and being fat, we still don't know why people who eat the same kinds and amounts of food come in different sizes. It seems likely that it's a combination of heredity, early metabolism, and activity levels, and it also seems likely that not all heavier people eat more than their lighter counterparts.

Not everyone who is fat is a compulsive eater. Not everyone who is fat is using their weight to express tangled emotions. Not everyone who is fat wants to be thinner.

I have written this book, not because I believe it's better to be thinner, but because I have experienced the anguish of revolving my life around food. It is not to the people that are large and living fully that I speak, but to the people who, at any weight, are using food as a substitute for participating in their lives.

My hope is that the book will inspire you to treat yourself and your eating with insight and compassion and that this insight and compassion will in turn extend to everyone you touch.

Most of all, I wish you a breaking free of your own.

Geneen Roth
Santa Cruz, California

1

Being Hungry Is Like Being in Love: If You Don't Know, You're Probably Not

'In all my adult life, I can remember only two times that I ate because I was actually hungry.'

A Breaking Free workshop participant

A few years ago during the third or fourth meeting of a Breaking Free workshop, one of the participants came in exasperated with herself, with the workshop, with me. She said, 'Eating when you're hungry is just another fad, just another diet some doctor made up. It's ridiculous.' There was a murmur of nervous laughter in the room, then silence. She continued, 'First one diet tells you to eat only certain combinations of fruit. Another tells you to eat protein. Then another tells you to eat a diet high in carbohydrates. Now *you're* telling me something else. This isn't any different from every other diet I've been on for the past fifteen years.' And she glowered at me, angry and confused.

I didn't blame her for being angry. I didn't blame her for feeling that she had been handed so many contrasting bits of information about food for so many years that she couldn't distinguish the ones that made sense from the ones that didn't. She was angry because I had told her to eat when she was hungry. Years of dieting had taught her not to trust her body's messages. After fifteen years of dieting, she had forgotten that eating had anything to do with being hungry.

She and the rest of the twenty million people in the United States who are on a diet at any given moment. From the time we cry as babies and our mothers, not knowing what we need, give us a cracker, the connection between our eating and hunger has grown more tenuous. So tenuous that the most natural way to eat – when we are hungry – sounds like just another fad.

The diets I followed were studded with rules: Never eat after 10:00 P.M., don't snack, eat two pieces of bread a day, don't eat bread, breakfast should be the biggest meal, breakfast should be the smallest meal, etc. Not one diet of the twenty-five or so I've been on mentioned eating when I was hungry.

By the time I was twenty-eight I knew how many calories were in any food that was presented to me. I knew how to lose weight and how to gain weight. I knew how to maintain my weight. I knew how to diet and how to binge. But I didn't know when I was hungry. More painful, I didn't know it was *okay* to be hungry. No one ever told me, or if they did, I had forgotten that being hungry was natural.

My body was my enemy. It was round instead of straight. My legs were short; my hips were wide. I had no ankles to speak of. The only straight, thin part of me was my hair, which I wanted to be thick and curly. I had a face like a moon, eyes that were too close together, eyebrows that didn't accentuate anything. My body had betrayed me, and I could not trust its messages.

A woman in a Breaking Free workshop says:

I was eating in a Mexican restaurant with a friend. After we shared a dinner of enchiladas with green sauce, guacamole, tortilla chips, and beer, I excused myself. On the way to the bathroom, my twenty-year-old chant repeated itself: 'I can't believe you ate so much. And so fattening. How many calories in an enchilada? Those tortilla chips were fried, why did you have to eat so many? You know fried isn't good for your liver. And on top of everything, you had to go and have a beer. At least you could have spared yourself the extra calories of alcohol. Your legs are already rubbing together.' On the way back from the bathroom I looked at my now-protruding stomach and asked myself how full I was. Not how fat I felt – because my mind had calculated every bite of food in my Weight Watcher mentality and compared it to what it thought I *should* have eaten – no, I was speaking directly to my body and asking it how it felt, how it actually felt with the amount of food I had put into it. I stopped right where I was – in the aisle beside two people who looked like they were on their third margarita each – when I realized that my body felt absolutely fine about what I had eaten. It wasn't too full or too empty, it didn't feel like grease from the chips was sloshing around in its veins. It hadn't turned into a tree sloth during the past thirty minutes. It didn't lumber or ooze over the sides of my pants. My body, in fact, was singing about the meal I had fed it. It was hungry, I had fed it, and it was very glad.

Suddenly I realized what a relief it was to have something physical, something *real* on which I could base what I eat – instead of mental images of what my body could look like if only I would eat less of this, more of that. Mental calculations based on an image of a body I could *never* have, regardless of whether I'd eaten anything different at any time of the day, week, month, or year. Not that what I eat doesn't more or less affect the shape of my body. But I've learned that my body does not shape itself according to my mental image.

Most of the time we eat in response to our minds. Most of the time we feed our bodies without consulting our bodies. Most of the time *when* we eat has little to do with *what* we are eating for – physical nourishment, satisfaction, a healthy body. Eating when we're hungry implies trusting the wisdom of our bodies; ultimately, it necessitates believing that our bodies know their appropriate weight better than we.

Those of us who have spent months or years or decades dieting learn that someone else always knows better and that if we listen to what they tell us to eat, we will have the body they tell us we'll have. Unappetizing, unattractive, and at times nauseating combinations of food become palatable if they promise slender arms and legs.

When inevitably we break from the confinement of a diet we are no closer to eating from hunger than we were when we were dieting. Now we eat something because we weren't allowed to eat it before, because we saw someone eating it when we were dieting, because we didn't eat it as a kid, because it's in the window and it looks good. We are still eating from external cues that have little to do with the body's need for a particular food at a particular time. When we diet we are taught to ignore hunger. When we're not dieting, we feel so deprived from ignoring our hunger that we try to make up for it by eating so much we don't allow ourselves to get hungry.

The first step in breaking free from compulsive eating is to eat when you are hungry. ①

Think back on the last time you ate. Did you look at your watch to see if it was time to eat? Did you have an appointment for lunch or dinner? Did you pass by a window with something luscious displayed and decide you couldn't pass it up? Were you hungry? How did you know?

When I first decided that I wasn't going to diet anymore, I began keeping a chart of when I ate, what I ate, and if I was hungry. After a few days I was dismayed to realized that I *never* ate because I was hungry. There were too many other good reasons to eat: when I was upset and needed a treat; when I was happy and needed to celebrate; when I was sad and needed to be comforted; when I was angry and didn't express it; when I was in love and wanted to share. And, if none of the above applied, when I was frustrated or bored and couldn't figure out what else to do. Eating when I was hungry sounded good, but the best part about food was eating when I wasn't hungry. Food was the glue that held my life together *between* hungers.

I didn't want to give up food; I relied on it too much. On the other hand, I was miserable with my body and with the overstated importance of food in my life. I knew I was absolutely not willing to go on another diet, so I decided that I would try eating when I was hungry. I told myself that if it was too hard to eat when I was hungry and if I was more unhappy doing that than with the consequences of eating whenever I wanted, I could stop any time.

I began by trying to quit eating long enough to get hungry. Which wasn't easy. After so many years of dieting (and not eating when I was hungry), then bingeing (and not eating when I was hungry), I wasn't sure my body knew what hunger was.

Giving up dieting, and breaking away from someone else's advice, rules and regulations about eating can be frightening. I remember the exhilaration of throwing away my scales and charts and lists of 'legal' foods. And I remember the terror that followed. It was as if I had been travelling in a tiny circle for years and suddenly someone said, 'Now you can go anywhere you want. You can go to the ocean, to the mountains, to the forest,' and I got scared. I knew I was tired of circling but I didn't know how to do anything else. I didn't know if I could.

When we give up dieting, we take back something we were often too young to know we had given away: our own voice. Our ability to make decisions about what to eat and when. Our belief in ourselves. Our right to decide what goes into our mouths. Unlike the diets that appear monthly in magazines or the thermal pants that sweat off pounds, unlike a lover or a friend or a car, your body is reliable. It doesn't go away, get lost, stolen. If you will listen, it will speak.

Part of breaking free is going from not listening to listening. Or from listening-to-everyone-else to listening-to-yourself. And trusting what you hear.

We have so many fears about hunger: if we wait, we might never get hungry; if we only eat when we are hungry, we won't get to eat all that we want or we will eat everything that isn't tied down. You can't talk yourself out of those fears. But you can experiment with them and discover if they are true.

I remember talking to my friend Sara as I was ending an intimate relationship and telling her how frightened I was about being alone again for what seemed like an endless stretch of nights ahead. She said, 'When you are here, in a night, you'll be able to deal with the loneliness. You can take a bath, read a book, cry, call me. You can deal with the loneliness one night at a time. But what you can't deal with is the *idea* of loneliness, the fear of it.'

The fear of hunger, like the fear of loneliness, seems to be connected with emptiness, echoes, endless wanting.

The experience of hunger is immediate, is sound and sensation.

You begin eating when you are hungry by letting yourself get hungry. When you are accustomed to eating in anticipation of hunger, making the transition to eating when you are hungry may require some time.

Here are a few suggestions to facilitate the change. It is important to remind yourself, both in this chapter and the ones to follow, that if you are using food as I was, and sometimes still do, to fill in the empty spaces, to deal with situations or feelings that are difficult to feel or act on, then the thought of doing these exercises may evoke anger or fear or resistance in you. You might not know what to do *instead* of eating; it might seem that there *is* nothing to do but eat or fall apart. The intensity of such reactions is understandable. If the feelings and/or situations for which you were using food weren't scary or uncomfortable or painful, you wouldn't have turned to food to allay them. If you eat only when you are hungry, or even think about eating when you are hungry, you are removing your protection from those feelings. Be patient with yourself. You need to find a balance between allowing your feelings to surface and taking yourself to the edge of what's comfortable. Until you move to that edge, you can't see what's beyond it. But that doesn't mean it's going to feel good or be easy all the time.

Look over the exercises. Do the ones that appeal to you first. Then go back over the ones that don't. What is it about them that you don't like? Is there something about yourself that you don't want to know? Do the exercises remind you of anything you've tried to do before and have 'failed' at?

● **Keep a chart of what you ate, the times at which you ate and whether or not you were hungry before you ate.** The importance of a chart is that it reveals your patterns with food exactly as they are and not how you imagine them to be. It's very easy to lie to yourself about food: a lick here, a fingerful there, it doesn't count if it's off someone else's plate. I often tell the participants in my workshops that they can think of the chart as a road map: You can't get to your destination if you don't know where you are.

First notice how you feel about keeping a chart. Does

it bring you back to your dieting days? Do you feel as though you're being imprisoned or monitored by an external authority? Do you feel you have to hide the chart so someone won't find it? Notice the entire range of your feelings – resistance, anger, rebellion. Let yourself go through them and keep a chart anyway.

After a few days of keeping the chart, how do you feel about eating? Do you want to 'be good' so that you don't have to write down what you eat when you are 'bad'? Do you forget to write down the times you eat when you aren't hungry? Whose voice do you hear reprimanding you for eating when you are not hungry?

And what about your actual food intake? Do you eat at scheduled times? Are you in touch with your body's need for food at those times?

How often do you eat when you are hungry?

Do you know what hunger feels like?

● **Don't eat at your regular meal times for a day or two, and if you find that it helps you get in touch with your hunger, try not eating at your regular times for a week or longer.**

If, for instance, you eat breakfast as soon as you wake up, without giving yourself the chance to get hungry, wait a little while. Watch what happens.

Are you anticipating your hunger?

Do you *want* to be hungry before you actually get hungry?

If you work at a nine to five job where you don't have the flexibility to take a meal break when you get hungry (i.e., at 10:30 A.M.), but you aren't hungry before you leave in the morning, bring some food with you so that when you do get hungry, you won't feel stranded or frightened. If you are not hungry at lunch, take a walk, read, do some errands, and, again, have some food in your desk that you can eat when you do get hungry.

If you live alone or in a situation that allows you meal-time flexibility, notice what, if anything, starts happening to you around dinnertime. Do you feel you should be eating? Do you feel you would be missing out on something important if you didn't eat dinner? Are there certain emotions that seem to surface at dinnertime? What does eating dinner alone mean to you?

For those who live with others, dinner can be difficult to rearrange because of its social significance. If it's too hard for you to change your evening meal plans, don't. Work with breakfast and lunch, but check in with yourself at dinner to see if you are hungry.

You don't have to do or decide anything about yourself and your hunger. For the time being, just watch. Notice where you are on the map.

● **Pay careful attention to the bodily sensations that you recognize as hunger.** When you feel yourself starting to get hungry, sit down for a few minutes (and if you can't sit down, stand still). Where in your body do you experience hunger? In your throat? Your chest? Your stomach? Your legs? How is this sensation different from the sensation, let's say, of excitement? Or loneliness?

What happens to you when you feel yourself getting hungry?

Do you feel that you need to eat immediately?

● **When you've decided you are hungry, rate your hunger on a scale of 1 to 10.*** Rating your hunger numerically provides objective criteria with which to compare past hunger and present hunger. It gives you direct access to an experience that is very sub-

* I'd like to thank Joy Imboden for her *Thin Within* programme, where I was first introduced to this scale.

jective and laden with emotional overtones. The low end of the scale can be used to signify 'ravenous, very hungry,' to 'medium,' to 'just-a-little-hungry.' Five is comfortable; at 6, you're starting to get full. When you hit 10, you're up to your neck in food.

When you start getting hungry, ask yourself where on the scale the hunger is located. At 5 or above, you probably want to be hungry more than you actually are.

Notice the number at which you feel most comfortable eating and the point at which your hunger is uncomfortable.

● **When you are not hungry and decide to eat, choose a food that you ate that day when you were hungry. Be aware of:**

1. how the food tastes
2. how the taste was different when you were hungry
3. if you enjoy it as much as when you were hungry
4. what, since it's not hunger, you are feeling
5. how you know when to stop eating

In working with hunger – my own and the participants in Breaking Free workshops – I've found that the following themes, fears, questions about hunger are raised again and again:

If I eat when I'm hungry, I'll eat all the time. (Or, I'll gain fifty pounds; I'll be obese; no one will love me.)

This feeling is the logical outcome of years of being conditioned to believe that our bodies lie, that they cannot be trusted, that they will betray us. Underlying the diet mentality, which is the one that most of us have internalized as the Truth, is the assumption that if you don't eat at regulated times you won't be able to regulate yourself.

Try to step outside yourself and observe how frightening it must be to believe that this body you walk around in, this mechanism on which you rely to move, to talk, to perform intricate tasks, to make love – this body is, at the very moment you let down your guard, ready to betray you. Why should you trust anything if you can't trust what is closest to you? And yet, who of all the women you know trusts her body to give her messages that will, when acted upon, serve to nourish rather than destroy her?

This lack of trust runs deep and is obviously complex. Because we have been brainwashed into accepting the body that newspapers, television, magazines, and movies idealize, and because we in turn have begun to believe that the shape of our bodies is ultimately within our control, our bodies become the battleground for an often lifelong and very intense contest of wills: its against ours. If we're unfortunate enough to be born into this culture without developing this culture's ideal body, and if, as women, we feel that the shape of our bodies determines our acceptance or rejection in both our professional and personal lives, and if we believe that we can use our will and our denial of bodily messages to shape our bodies, then the struggle is endless. There is always the body that is crying out for more food and the mind that is crying out for more weight loss. We learn to treat our bodies like naughty children whose wishes are absolutely out of the question. We learn to judge them, ignore them, ridicule them, torture them.

We eat what the current authority tells us to eat, when we are told to eat it. And because the current authority is usurped monthly by a *more* current authority, what and when we feed ourselves also changes – and often.

Your body gets hungry. When you feed it, it gets satisfied. There is no magic about it. It might take a while to sift through the various sensations you feel and distinguish hunger from sadness or loneliness, but that's because you're not used to recognizing hunger – and *not* because your body doesn't feel it or because your hunger, if you let yourself recognize it, would be insatiable. No one has to tell you when to eat; your body will tell you. No one *can* tell you when to eat; they aren't in touch with your stomach. And if you are listening to your body to tell you when to eat, you can also hear it saying 'enough.'

How do I know when I am hungry? Not by the clock, not by food's looking or smelling good, not by a previously arranged lunch or dinner date. You know when you are hungry because your body starts telling you, gently at first, then in no uncertain voice, that it needs food and it needs it now. You know when you are hungry because you start feeling that if you don't get food quickly, you will bite into someone's arm. You know you are hungry the way you know you have to pee. Because there's no mistaking the signals.

There are different stages of hunger, and hunger feels a little different for each person. I know I'm beginning to get hungry when I feel a certain queasiness. Usually, I wait to eat until I am hungrier. Hungrier means that the queasy sensation gets stronger, followed by contractions and growling in my abdomen. If I don't eat at this point, I begin to get irritable, lightheaded . . . I feel I would do anything to get food and would eat anything I could get my hands on.

But that is *my* hunger pattern. You need to discover your own.

If I only eat when I'm hungry, I won't be able to eat as much as I want or when I want it. That's true.

But the amount that you want is often not as much as your body wants. Ask yourself what you are feeling and why you want to eat more than your body needs. What is it that you want from food beyond its nourishing your body?

While it is true that eating nourishes you visually, tactilely, olfactorily, it does these best when you are hungry. When you are not hungry, you are using food 'to glue your life together between hungers.' It's fine to do that if you are aware of what you are doing; it's even fine to continue doing that if you are willing to accept (and I mean *really* accept) having a larger-than-ideal body.

Do you want to eat as much as you want more than you want to change how you deal with food and feel about your body? There is *nothing wrong* with either a yes or no answer, but at some level, it is a choice you have to make again and again. When you walk in the door from work on a busy day there is an in-between time, a string of moments when you don't know what to do with yourself, so you open the refrigerator. You want to eat, it would taste good, but you're not hungry. And you can't think of anything to do that sounds as good as eating. That's the moment where the choice has to be made. Again.

One night when I was by myself, reading a book, I suddenly got an overwhelming yearning for chocolate. In less than two minutes, I had put on my coat, picked up my keys and was opening the door in a mad rush for a Cadbury's Fruit and Nut Bar (the large size). As I stepped outside, I asked myself if I was hungry. 'No,' came the answer. I decided that I would go back inside, sit down, and spend a few minutes examining why I wanted the chocolate and what I wanted it to do. If, afterward, I still wanted chocolate, I told myself I could buy it. At times like these, I find it helpful to go through a dialogue with myself, using a questioning and an answering voice and either talking out loud (if I'm alone) or carrying on the dialogue very distinctly in my head. That night it went something like this:

ME: What's going on?
MYSELF: I'm feeling lonely. I want to be held. I want chocolate.
ME: What do you think chocolate will do?
MYSELF: Well, there's no one around and chocolate is better than nothing. It tastes good.
ME: Does chocolate have arms and legs?
MYSELF: Very funny.
ME: Does it?
MYSELF: No.
ME: Can it hold you?
MYSELF: No.

I realized that I was going to feel just as lonely after the chocolate as before, that what I really wanted was for it to be cuddly and to hug. Once I became certain about what I wanted the food to do, it was clear the chocolate wasn't the answer. So I took a bath and went to bed.

The striking thing about this incident is that I *didn't know* I was lonely until I had decided to buy chocolate.

When you want food and you're not hungry, it's a good indicator that you want something less tangible but don't know what it is or else feel that you might not be able to get it. So while it's true that if you eat when you're hungry you won't always eat when you want, it is also true that you can use the desire to eat when you are not hungry as an indicator that you need something less material than food and that until you stop eating you cannot discover what that might be.

When I'm not hungry and good food is around, I feel that I'm missing something very special if I don't eat. This feeling – the fear of missing something that might be marvellous and unrepeatable – often arises at parties, restaurants, family dinners, and holidays: any place, any time at which a lot of people are congregated over a lot of food. I feel it often when I decide not to go somewhere (a party, a concert, a new city) or participate in an event (a lecture, a workshop) that seems to promise excitement, new people, growth. When I worry about what I might be or am missing, I forget the reasons I decided not to go, reasons that stem from an awareness of what I need at that point: quiet time, alone time, sleep. It's hard to say no; why not push myself a little more? What if it turns out that this is the workshop that could have changed my life or at which I would have met my lifetime partner? What if that chocolate mousse is the most ecstatic of all ecstasies?

At a potluck dinner we had in a Breaking Free workshop, I was sitting across the room from a woman who had 'I am beyond full' written on her face. She had unbuttoned her slacks and was slouched to one side so that her stomach could sit on the other side. I watched her look at the table of food, decide something, then take her plate and walk over to the cheesecake. When she sat back down with her new treasure, she caught my eye and we both laughed. I asked her if she was full. 'Very,' she said.

'Why are you eating cheesecake?'

'Because when I saw the cheesecake walk in, I thought, "I'm gonna wanna have some."'

I was gonna wanna have some but now I am full and I really can't taste anything anymore but it looks so good, I don't want to miss the taste of it. What difference does it make that I might be so full I can't sleep and that I'll wake up in the morning wishing tonight had never happened? What difference does it make that I will hate myself afterward?

When you are not hungry and good food is around, what you miss by not eating is food that never tastes as good as it does when you are hungry. You miss that particular cheesecake BUT you can: (a) ask to take a piece home; (b) ask for the recipe; (c) go out tomorrow when you *are* hungry and find the best cheesecake in town; (d) invite the cheesecake contributor to dinner and ask her to 'make something . . . why not dessert . . . how about cheesecake?'

When you are not hungry and good food is around, what you *do* miss by eating is the chance to take care of yourself, to see that the world won't end if you don't eat the cheesecake. You miss the chance not to get sick, to be so full you can't sleep, and to wake up in the morning wishing the night had never happened.

When you are not hungry enough to begin eating or too full to continue, you miss the taste of food anyway. It's like going to a movie when you want to be asleep, going to a party when you want to be alone, going to a workshop when you want to be walking on the beach. When, for any number of reasons, your attention is not present (because of the full sensations in your body or a strong desire to be elsewhere) you miss the experience.

If my lifetime partner were at a lecture I pushed myself to attend, my vision of him would be skewed. Upon meeting him, I'd probably pick on something about him that rubbed me the wrong way: I'd notice that the third finger of his left hand had dirt under the nail (doesn't he ever wash his hands?). Or I'd think his ears were too big. I could meet my lifetime partner at a lecture and be so tired that I'd look away and leave, never knowing that I left Mr Right Enough behind.

I'm afraid to let myself get hungry; I feel so empty. The sensation of hunger is sometimes accom-

panied by a corresponding physical sensation of emptiness and hollowness. The sounds of hunger are hollow
sounds: growling, rumbling. If we are fearful of allowing ourselves to need, if we fear that those needs, if
expressed, might never be met, the sensation of hunger
can evoke the emotion of hunger. Because it is an emotion that is repressed, we push it away; we don't want to
be reminded of it. When physical hunger activates our
yearning or wanting or aching, we feel frightened.

Some feelings are frightening. And we make them
worse by being frightened because we're frightened.
The feelings of emptiness will come and they will go.
Yearning will come and it will pass. If you don't allow
feelings, if you push them away, they get bigger, become
more threatening. Feelings don't go away because
you're afraid of them.

Physical hunger is of the body. Physical hunger asks
for food. Non-physical hunger is of the mind, the heart.
When you see that your physical hunger is capable of
being fulfilled, you can begin to allow that same possibility for your emotional hunger.

When you don't allow yourself hunger, you don't
allow yourself satisfaction.

2
Deciding What You Want to Eat: Having Your Cake and Eating It, Too

'I ate a piece of cake in front of God and everyone.'

A Breaking Free workshop participant

On that day, five years ago, when I decided I could eat anything I wanted without guilt and would never diet again, visions of chocolate chip cookies appeared. Homemade, warm from the oven, the chips melting into one another. I went to the store, bought a bag of bittersweet chocolate chips, flour, sugar, eggs, and butter. My heart pounded as I wheeled the shopping cart from aisle to aisle. I kept looking around to see if anyone was pointing at me, whispering about me, ready to report me to my mother or to my leader at Weight Watchers. I thought about putting a head of lettuce in the cart to make it look as if I were shopping for salad fixings and had decided to make cookies for the kids as a treat. Then I realized I'd have to get tomatoes and radishes (I don't like radishes) and that seemed like going too far, so I paid for my groceries and left. I could not remember a time when I had *allowed* myself to eat cookies. When I binged I felt as if I were sneaking behind my own back and later on, or tomorrow, I would be caught and have to pay the consequences. When I binged I ate quickly, often standing in front of the refrigerator, and if I heard anyone coming, I hid what I was eating immediately.

This was different. I was living with my friend Lucy

and her daughter and I was going to make the cookies right in front of them.

Which is exactly what I did. Lucy cooked a pot roast and mashed potatoes for her dinner. We sat down at the same time, lit the candles, put our napkins in our laps. She began with her salad, moved to the carrots, and finished with the meat and potatoes. I began with one cookie, moved on to the second, and finished with the fourth. We both ate ice cream for dessert.

The next day, when I asked myself what I wanted, a roll of chocolate chip cookie dough came floating into my mind. Cutting it into thick slices and eating it. Raw chocolate chip cookie dough. Okay, I thought, if that's what you want . . . I went back to the store, bought another bag of chocolate chips, threw a supercilious glance toward the vegetable department, and left. For lunch, I ate a few balls of dough. At dinner, Lucy and I went through the ritual of lighting the candles, putting our napkins in our laps, smiling at each other, and then eating. On her plate was eggplant casserole and salad. On my plate were five chocolate chip cookies, two cooked and three raw. Both of us were too full for dessert.

The next day's meal plan was the same. And the next. And the next. For two weeks I ate chocolate chip cookies in various shapes and consistencies for breakfast, lunch, dinner, and in-between. On the fourth day of the second week, I ate an egg for lunch. For dinner on the fourteenth day, I ate some lasagne that Lucy had made. And a ball of dough for variety. On the fifteenth day, I never wanted to see a chocolate chip cookie again.

I tell this story at the beginning of every workshop because it's absurd and because it's true. I tell it because almost everyone there has fantasized about eating as much as she wants of whatever she wants without feeling guilty and few people will allow themselves this freedom (or this madness). Not that two weeks of uninterrupted chocolate-chip-cookie-consumption was all pleasure. Or even mostly pleasure. I wondered if anyone ever got cancer from eating fifteen dozen chocolate chip cookies. I wondered if my brain cells were dying from lack of nourishment. I wondered what kind of ridiculous idea had gotten into my head, what made me think I could decide for myself what I wanted to eat. My pants were getting tighter; I had gained weight and I was frightened that I'd keep gaining. But I had promised myself to eat exactly what I wanted, believing that eventually my body's natural wisdom would surface. I didn't know how long it would take but I was willing to find out. After seventeen years of dieting and bingeing, seventeen years of losing and gaining weight, I figured that if it took another six months and another fifteen pounds to begin to trust myself, it would be well worth the wait. And if it were not true, if I could not decide for myself what to eat without destroying myself, then I would be no worse off than before: For the umpteenth time in my life, I would have twenty pounds to lose.

It was worth the wait.

At first I couldn't imagine what would make me stop wanting chocolate chip cookies. And then I couldn't imagine wanting another.

After cookies, I began to crave vegetables. Not often, but enough so that I stopped worrying about my brain cells. Whenever I was hungry, and often when I wasn't, I'd ask myself what I wanted to eat, and then, as frequently as possible, I ate it. I went through phases of ice cream, pizza, hot dogs, popcorn, chocolate. Although I wasn't aware of it at the time, I was craving a lot of the foods I had deprived myself of through the years. Everything but Hostess Sno-balls, which, as fondly as I remembered them as a child, were too pink for me to eat as an adult.

The chocolate-chip-cookie stint took place in November. By May I had gained fifteen pounds. From May through September, my weight stabilized. In October, still eating what I wanted, I began to lose weight, and over the next two years, I lost thirty pounds. That was five years ago. Depending on the time of year, my weight now fluctuates about twelve pounds.

One of the reasons it's terrifying for compulsive eaters to believe we can eat what we want and not become obese is that we think we want so much. We think we still want what we weren't allowed as a child, as a teenager, as a young adult. We think we want what we couldn't have last year or last month or yesterday. We may feel so deprived from all that we once wanted and couldn't have that when the option of eating what we want is suggested, our well of deprivation seems huge. We feel bottomless, as if we could never get enough. We try to make up for the years of dieting in two weeks of chocolate chip cookies or a month-long binge. Until we realize we are grown-ups. When I looked at the package of Hostess Sno-balls and told myself I really could have them if I wanted them, I realized I *did* want them . . . when I was ten years old. Then, they were a treat. Now I knew that they were nothing more than pink-covered imitation chocolate cake and imitation marshmallow cream. Now I could think of a better treat. And now, if I wasn't hungry, I could treat myself to something as comforting as, but not necessarily, food.

Two weeks of chocolate chip cookies did not make up for all the times I had said 'No thank you, I don't want one' when I wanted one more than anything else I could think of. A triple scoop of rocky road ice cream every day for a month could not compensate for the years of passing by ice cream parlours and wishing I could be a normal person who walked up to the counter and asked for a cone without feeling the wrath of God would descend upon me. I could eat from morning till night for the next six months or six years and I would have still dieted and binged for seventeen years of my life.

There isn't enough food in the world to heal the isolation of those years. There isn't enough food to fill the space created by the deprivation and the ensuing feelings of craziness.

We can't go back. We can't eat for all the times we didn't eat. We *can* use that pain as an indicator of what doesn't work. We don't have to deprive ourselves any longer. Beginning today.

A balance exists, however, between not depriving yourself of the food you want when you are hungry and using food to make up for all the other ways you feel deprived. All the ways you can't have what you want. The flip side of feeling that you have to eat cottage cheese and carrot sticks because if you let yourself eat mashed potatoes or quiche you'd gain weight is eating mashed potatoes or quiche every time you feel like it because there are so many other things in your life you want and can't have, you'll be damned if you'll deprive yourself of this too. Eating what you want gets translated to eating whenever you want regardless of your hunger, and it is not long before the eating gets out of control and you fulfil your own prophecy: You can't eat what you want because when you do, you gain weight.

There is no end to wanting. You pass a bakery, smell fresh bread. You want some. Your friend is eating butterfly shrimp, you ordered chicken. Hers looks better. You want it. Magazines, TV commercials, newspapers are filled with endless varieties of clothes, cars, vacation spots, equipment that promise to make us happier, more beautiful. We want them. And if we have enough money, we can buy them. But there are some things we want that we will never be able to have. The perfect relationship, job, children, parents, friends. We are not in control of having these things the way we want them, but we are in control of what we eat. Consequently, we turn to and use food as the area in our lives in which we can have exactly what we want when we want it. And when we gain weight, our belief in ourselves is diminished. The diet authorities must be right, we tell ourselves, we cannot lose weight by listening to ourselves. We cannot be trusted.

And while it is true that you cannot trust the feeling that because you want something you must have it, it is not true that *you* cannot be trusted. Or that you cannot lose weight by listening to yourself.

I want a cheese enchilada and guacamole. Now. I've been at my desk writing for a few hours and I'm a little tired and I could use a break. I'm not hungry, but that doesn't take away the desire to eat. At least not right now. If I got up from my desk, drove to a Mexican restaurant, and ate an enchilada, I would probably enjoy it. At the very least, it would be a welcome relief from writing. I would enjoy being away from my desk – moving, driving, seeing people, talking. That I want to eat when I am not hungry does not translate to 'I cannot trust what I want.'

Trust develops and builds when I am given a choice (and not, as in dieting, denied it). Trust develops when I choose to make myself comfortable, not miserable, to take care of myself rather than hurt myself.

Trust develops when you learn from actual experience that you can decide which desires to act upon and which you will leave to fantasy.

There is no end to wanting. After the enchilada, I

might walk down the street and pass an ice cream parlour. I might want a sundae. And after that, I might see someone eating a chocolate bar and want one myself. There is always the next thing to want. And the next.

It is the nature of our minds to want what promises satisfaction. There is nothing unusual or untrustworthy about that. What is unusual is that instead of being taught that of course we will want endlessly, we're taught that because we do want, there must be something wrong and we have to watch ourselves vigilantly. The only crazy thing about wanting to eat when we are not hungry is not expecting to want to eat when we are not hungry.

When you decide to eat and then decide what you will eat, the first question to ask yourself is, 'Where is the desire to eat coming from?' The second question is, 'Where is the desire for this particular food coming from?' If the answer to the first question is that you are hungry, you might now examine the steps you can take in choosing to eat a particular food at a particular time.

Forget about calories. This suggestion and each of the following ones, as well as all the exercises in the book, are based on the premise that you will give yourself permission to eat from as wide a selection of foods as is physically and economically available to you. That means anything from Sara Lee to Pepperidge Farm, Cadbury's, Haagen-Dazs, nearby gourmet delicatessen and bake shops, pasta, potatoes, rice, bread. Anything you've been denying yourself since childhood, last year, last month, yesterday that you want now. That means no forbidden foods.* That means nothing is too fattening. It makes no difference if a hard boiled egg has 78 or

---

* Those on medically restricted diets need to adjust these suggestions for their particular cases.

88 calories. The question is: Do you want a hard boiled egg? Because if you don't want it and you eat it, you won't be satisfied. Chances are you'll go grazing for more food. Chances are you'll find more. Chance are you'll begin with low-caloric nibbles and eat your way through the medium-caloric to the high-caloric foods in a short time. If you want lasagne and eat a hard boiled egg, chances are you'll end up eating two or three times the calories you would have had you begun with the lasagne.

We eat so that we can continue to move, breath, talk. We eat because we have to eat to stay alive. But we choose certain foods over others for a variety of reasons. Sometimes we want and need to feel fuller, heavier, warmer, so we eat protein, hot foods, spicy foods. Sometimes we want to feel lighter; sometimes we feel that we need something cold, something that will go down easily, so we choose fruit or an iced drink. We eat, even when we are hungry, to satisfy emotional as well as physical needs. Certain foods match certain moods or situations. When I am lonely and hungry, I often want a baked potato. There is something about its whiteness, its fluffiness, and its warmth that comforts me. At other times, I want vanilla ice cream because it is creamy and smooth and fills me up. At those times I want something that will coat my stomach. At those times, I need a kind of filling up that vanilla ice cream seems to produce. My friend Sue eats meat loaf, peas, and mashed potatoes when she is sad. Her mother often fixed that for their family when she was growing up, and now, when she is hungry and needs comforting, eating that particular meal helps her. 'But it has to be frozen peas,' she says, 'like my mother used. Otherwise it won't work.'

Diets do not give you the option of eating frozen peas and mashed potatoes when you are lonely. Diets, based on caloric consumption, do not leave room for being lonely. Or sad or angry or joyful. Diets exclude our psychological and emotional needs by assuming that we are going to feel the same way about ourselves, our relationships, our lives, on day one as on day six. Diets exclude all feelings except for those of wanting to be thin. Diets remove from us one of the few characteristics that distinguishes us from other animals – choice.

The main reason we are frightened when told that we can eat what we want is because we don't believe it. Not really. There is still a voice that says, 'Well, maybe a cookie, but not ice cream. Not bread. Think of the calories. Think of the weight you'll gain. Don't eat those things. You can't.' After years of counting calories and being told what to eat, we have evolved a rigid definition of what is permissible to eat and what is not: Low-caloric foods are all that is permissible.

A woman in my group says, 'For as long as I can remember, I was *supposed* to be on a diet.' When she wasn't eating dietetic foods, she was feeling guilty. When she was eating dietetic foods, she wished she wasn't.

In my continuing groups, in which the members have participated in at least one and sometimes two or three Breaking Free workshops, a constant observation is, 'I still feel as if I shouldn't be allowed to eat fattening food.' Not allowed. So that when they do, they feel as if they're breaking a law, doing what's forbidden. Eating what they want means indulging. Translated to: 'When I give myself what I need or want, I am doing something wrong.'

As long as there is that voice of 'not allowed,' as long as there are foods you feel you shouldn't eat, you create struggle and conflict. As long as there is struggle, there is bingeing. And as long as there is bingeing, there is fear about eating what you want.

You can't eat what you want and still lose weight

because you don't truly eat what you want. You eat in accordance with the Voice or in rebellion against it. *But that voice is not your voice.* It is the voice of whomever (your mother, lover, doctor) or whatever (any number of diets, articles, books) you have internalized. Over the years, you have come to believe it is not only your own voice but the correct one.

When you let go of the struggle by allowing yourself choice about what you eat, you let go of one end of the rope on which you have been tugging and straining. When you let go of your side, the rope immediately falls to the ground. War requires at least two sides. When you decide that you will listen to *yourself* and not to your calorie-counter or your fears, there is nothing to rebel against. There is nothing you can't have tomorrow so there is no reason to eat it all today.

During the years I spent agonizing about my weight, every day was a test of strength. If in the morning or afternoon I ate one 'wrong' or fattening food, even a bite, I felt as if I had blown it. So why not blow it for the rest of the day and start dieting tomorrow? I'd spend the day eating as much as I possibly could, storing up for the next day, when I knew I'd be deprived. I'd eat everything I had in the house then go to the store and buy large quantities of anything I wanted. At 11:59 P.M. I'd anticipate the midnight hour when tomorrow would begin. The next morning, I'd wake up feeling disgusted with myself and sick to my stomach.

On one such a morning I wrote:

The dawn is lovely and I don't care. I don't care about anything but how fat I am. I awaken with a huge stomach. My face looks like someone blew air into my cheeks, my body feels like someone poured a bottle of glue into it and filled me up until it reached my head. I am frightened, really frightened. I don't see how I am ever going to stop eating like this because as miserable as I am, I want to eat.

The cashew butter is in the pantry. A voice says, 'So you will diet tomorrow. What's one more day? You're going to lose twenty-five pounds anyway, you might as well eat. It's Wednesday. You can't diet until the end of the week, you'll be too weak to study.' And I think, 'Yeah, you're right. What's one more day?' I get up and walk toward the cashew butter. Then I think about how sick I am going to feel. How sick I already feel. And I refrain. For the moment. It's 7:00 A.M. and the struggle is on . . .

Back and forth. I forced myself into dieting, afraid that my hunger was so deep I could devour the world. When, inevitably, I binged, I felt I had given proof of that. At no point was I in touch with what I *wanted* to eat, only what I was allowed to eat and not allowed to eat. And no matter what else I had eaten and no matter how sick I felt, I wanted sweets. I was still, at twenty-eight, the child who was proving to her mother that 'I can too have frozen Milky Ways and if you say I can't, I'll sneak them into my pyjamas.'

A woman in my group said, 'I am amazed to discover that after forty years of bingeing on sugar, when I let myself eat what I want, I don't even *like* the taste of sweets.'

Most of us know how many calories are in apples, bread, meat, cheese. If knowing about and therefore eating by caloric content were what it takes to be thin, all of us would be thin.

In a moment of despair or sadness or anger, all that you know about calories (and all the reasons you want to be thin) will be swept away unless you are giving yourself the permission to eat. When you want to escape from a feeling, you will often do so by breaking a restriction you have imposed upon yourself. When you are in pain and want release, any kind of release will do, even when the release (breaking your diet) and the feeling you want release from (frustration or sadness) are unrelated. The urgency of emotion is far more powerful than the rational decision to consume 1,200 calories a day.

When you eat what you want, when you drop the rope and end the struggle between right foods and wrong foods, you will eventually (after your first tendency to eat more than you truly want) consume fewer calories than you did when you were guided by caloric content.

Your body wants to survive and it wants to be comfortable. It wants to be able to move, run, walk up the stairs with ease. When you drop the struggle, you can listen to that *and* eat what you want. Because what you will want is not only the freedom to choose what to eat but the freedom to have a body that performs fluidly and the freedom to like that body, as well as the self who inhabits it.

When you are hungry, sit down for a minute or two and ask yourself what you really want to eat. If no answer comes, either visually or verbally, the following list offers a variety of textures, tastes, and temperatures that you may consider:

Taste: Do you want something . . .
- sweet?
- sour?
- salty?
- spicy?
- bland?

Texture: Do you want something . . .
- smooth, that will slip down your throat?
- crunchy, that you really have to chew?

> • creamy, with substance, something that will fill your mouth up?
> • noisy, that pops and crackles when you chew?

Temperature: Do you want something . . .
> • hot and substantial or hot and liquidy, like tea or thin soup?
> • at room temperature (a piece of fruit, crackers, nuts)?
> • cold, and if so, do you want to drink it or eat it?

When you take the time to ask yourself these questions and to answer them, you'll have a much clearer indication of what will satisfy you than you do when you open the refrigerator and see what's there. You will be able to take part in the decision-making process about which restaurant to go to when you are eating out with friends or family.

Stay in the present moment with yourself. It will be tempting to decide what you are going to want to eat, or should eat, for breakfast, lunch, or dinner tomorrow when you are going to sleep at night. These decisions are not based on giving yourself permission to eat what you want but on preconceived ideas of what would be best for you or what would taste delicious. This is especially likely to happen when you see yourself losing weight without dieting. The reasoning goes: If I lost weight by eating cookies and ice cream, think how much more weight I would lose if I cut out the cookies. This kind of thinking is counterproductive. Whenever you notice yourself planning meals around what you should or shouldn't eat, or even around what you might want to eat, you are creating a set of expectations for yourself, which, if you don't meet them, will evoke the familiar feeling of weight-related failure. This feeling is the forerunner of a binge: You feel you've failed . . . you can't do *anything* right . . . you should have known this wasn't going to work . . . what's the use . . . you might as well eat. At the very least, deciding today what might taste delicious tomorrow is not allowing for any mood shifts or the inevitability of needs changing from day to day. When you eat what you thought you wanted yesterday and it doesn't satisfy you today, you'll go looking for more food.

What to do when you've started a meal and you realize it's not what you want. Last week, leaving my dance class, I visualized my lunch-to-be. It was a cold lunch, a salad with croutons and artichoke hearts. At home, I cut up the carrots, red pepper, cucumber, and lettuce, added the croutons and artichoke hearts. When I sat down and began to eat, I realized I didn't want it. I was cold and wanted something hot, something filling. But I had spent a long time chopping, shredding and preparing – and what about the starving children in India?

I looked down at the salad, picked up a carrot slice, remembered the last time I had prepared something I later didn't want and ate it anyway. A few weeks before, I had made a casserole for dinner, a very healthy casserole with vegetables and cheese and rice. After a bite or two, I realized I wanted ice cream and had been wanting it all day. Vanilla ice cream with flecks of vanilla bean on a crunchy sugar cone. No, I thought, I should eat this casserole, I haven't eaten vegetables all week. I'd get cold if I ate ice cream, it's too fattening anyway. So I ate the casserole, a salad, some bread. Afterward I ate two cookies and some licorice. Still unsatisfied, I went through a bowl of popcorn. Visions of vanilla ice cream wove in and out of my thoughts, mostly in.

Sometimes, when this happens the dialogue with myself goes: 'There are times when you can't eat everything you want when you want it. If you were more in touch, you would have gone for the ice cream, but since you're human and subject to mistakes, you didn't. So if you still want the ice cream tomorrow, you can have it, but right now, I'm going to sleep.' That night of the healthy casserole, however, I wanted ice cream. So, at ten in the evening – I had eaten dinner at six-thirty – I drove to the ice cream parlour and, physically full but emotionally unsatisfied, ordered what I had wanted three-and-a-half hours earlier.

Sitting with my salad, I remembered that I had been so full that night I had had difficulty falling asleep. I didn't want to make myself that uncomfortable again. So I put the salad away in a container, heated some soup and made a grilled cheese sandwich.

We eat to satisfy emotional as well as physical needs, and unless both are acknowledged and dealt with, we are setting ourselves up to feel deprived and go hunting for more food.

When you've sat down to a meal you realize you don't want:

● **Don't be ashamed to admit it to yourself.** Even if you don't act on the desire to eat something else, you will understand why you don't feel satisfied and, in some cases, this insight may be enough to prevent you from grazing for the next four hours. If you decide you can't or don't want to prepare or order more food, tell yourself that tomorrow, when you are hungry you will give yourself total permission to eat what you want. (You have to be telling the truth when you say this, otherwise it won't work.)

● **and you are alone, you can wrap up your meal and put it away.** If you don't already know what you want, take a few minutes to decide. And then, do what you can, either by preparing it or going out, to give it to yourself. You can eat the leftovers tomorrow or you can give them away to a friend, your dog, or the birds.

● **and you are at home with people with whom you feel relaxed, you can either say something like, 'I just realized I don't want this'; or, 'For some reason, this doesn't taste good or agree with me now'; or, if you don't feel you have to explain, you can take another plate and eat something else.** If someone asks what you are doing, tell them. There is no need to be ashamed; they may feel the same way, and if so, your honesty will relieve them and allow them to do the same.

● **and you are at a restaurant, you can:**

1. ask your companion(s) if they would like your dish. Or, if theirs appeals to you, if they are interested in trading.
2. ask the waiter or waitress to wrap up your food for taking and then order something else.
3. decide that next time you will take longer to choose what you want, but this time you will eat what you ordered and enjoy it as much as you can. If you are thoroughly unsatisfied by what you ordered, eat a little bit and when you go home, eat anything else you want.

A natural tendency when you first give yourself permission to eat what you want is to take that permission to an extreme and insist on getting the food you want no matter what. During my initial period of trial-by-choco-late-chip-cookies, I'd often change restaurants two or three and, occasionally, four times if I couldn't find exactly what I wanted. This was a bit trying for my friends, who wondered what absurd diet I had embarked on this time. Now I try to make the best possible choice, don't go anywhere I really don't want to go, and do the best with a restaurant or food that is not my first choice. In situations in which I cannot have exactly what I want, there are usually enough other kinds of nourishment (i.e., communication, intimacy, visual beauty) to satisfy the emotional level of eating. At those times, I put food into second priority and allow myself to be nourished by whatever is around me.

In the preceding four circumstances, the flexibility you allow yourself, the permission to feel what you feel, and the acknowledgement of these feelings is crucial. You may not choose to act on your feelings. That's fine. It's not always possible to eat what you want, but it is always possible to recognize and allow the disparity between what you are doing and what you'd like to be doing. When you give your feelings that much room and that much acceptance, you are no longer driven by an urgent but unconscious need to devour the world.

If it doesn't hum to you, don't eat it. Alyssa a woman who took a Breaking Free workshop with the goal of losing fifty pounds, told this story one night: 'When I got hungry on Wednesday night, I realized I wanted a truffle from India Joze. I told this to my husband who was eating steak and potatoes for dinner. He looked surprised but didn't criticize me for wanting chocolate that was fifteen miles away in the rain down a long windy road. Especially since I need to lose fifty pounds. After he finished his dinner, we drove to India Joze. I ordered a truffle, ate a few bites of it, and left most of it on my plate. I was satisfied. My husband, still cooperating, ate the rest. Then we drove back up the mountain in the rain. Laughing.'

The truffle hummed to Alyssa. Because it hummed, it satisfied her. And because it satisfied her, she didn't have to eat it all.

In *The Psychologist's Eat Anything Diet,* authors Lillian and Leonard Pearson use the words 'hummer' and 'beckoner' for foods we eat. Hummers are the foods you know you want *before* you see them; you can imagine their textures, tastes, and temperatures when they are not in front of you. Humming foods are specific; when you want cheese, an eclair will not do. They change according to the time of day, whom you are with, how you are feeling. Foods that hum to you are foods that satisfy you both emotionally and physically because they fit the hunger of the moment. And because they are so specific, they may not be convenient foods or those that are readily available. But they do the trick; they satisfy. When you eat a humming food, you don't go looking for more food fifteen minutes or an hour later. After you eat a humming food, you forget about food. You know those people who actually think about things other than food during the day? You become one of them.

Beckoning foods are what the name implies. A beckoner crooks its finger at you, draws you near, but because its attractiveness originates externally and does not correspond to a specific need or desire for that food, it is not satisfying. When you eat a beckoning food it's difficult to know when to stop because there isn't anything but the sight or smell or taste of it telling you to begin. When the hunger for food is absent, so is the signal that tells you to stop. Beckoning foods are usually convenient, readily available, and require little or no waiting or preparation. When you stand at the toaster popping the half-done bread out every few seconds, taking a bite and pushing it back down, that's called beckoning.

Most of us eat beckoning foods most of the time. What with TV, radio, and magazine ads, along with bakery windows, tempting descriptions or sights of food, and our own ideas about what we should and shouldn't eat, it is rare that we take the time to give ourselves permission to eat humming foods. The fear of eating what you want and gaining weight arises, the caloric consideration comes up, the feeling that you don't deserve to have what you want surfaces. Sometimes you don't know what you want; you've been eating certain foods with certain attitudes for so long that it may be quite a while before your true food preferences reveal themselves.

Rate the foods you eat according to their humming and beckoning qualities. Divide a piece of paper in three parts: Item, Hummer, Beckoner. Write down what you eat and then check whether that food is a hummer or a beckoner. Then rate the degree it hums to you on a scale of 1 to 10. Ten is humming loudly; 1 is a murmur. When you've done that for a week, change the scale to a beckoning scale. Use the same numbers, but this time, 10 is getting close to a hummer – you've thought about the food but possibly wouldn't have eaten it unless you heard about it, saw it, etc. One is as low as it goes – you aren't hungry, didn't give the food a moment's attention before you passed it by, smelled it.

Most of us don't take the time to discover what pleases us. This exercise not only gently pushes us into that discovery but also into the realization that we can give to ourselves *and* to others, that in fact we have more to give when we are giving to ourselves.

How often do you eat foods that you really want?

Make a list of 'forbidden' foods that you want, dream of, or think about, but haven't let yourself eat for years. Are there any childhood favourites that now seem silly as well as fattening? What about family favourites or ethnic foods that have specific associations for you? Have you cut those out of your diet? Continue the list until you've exhausted every possibility.

Then, list in hand, bring one forbidden food into your house each week. Bring more of it than you could eat in one sitting. When you are hungry, eat some of it and stay aware of how it tastes now. Is it really that good? Is it different from the taste you remembered or imagined? Do you want more?

A friend of mine craved packaged sugar cookies that she hadn't let herself eat since childhood. Every time she shopped at the market she'd glance at the rows of sweets, find the sugar cookies, decide no, she couldn't, wouldn't, and she'd move on. On my suggestion, she went to the store and bought three packages of sugar cookies. She called me half an hour later. 'You're not going to believe this,' she said. 'I don't even *like* them. For thirty years I've been dying for this moment and now they're not even good. *I* make better cookies.' We laughed, and she fed the cookies to the dog.

If the thought of eating what you want is overwhelming to you, begin very slowly, one meal at a time. When you awaken in the morning, give yourself permission to choose what you want for your first meal. After you've taken a few minutes to visualize what you want, prepare it, or go to the market and buy it, or to a restaurant and order it. Notice how you feel about something you wouldn't ordinarily allow yourself. Do you want to stop? What's the worst that could happen? If you're afraid you'll gain weight, don't pretend you're not afraid. At the same time, listen closely to your body.

When it tells you you've had enough (see Chapter 4), put down your fork, spoon, fingers. Now, how do you feel? Remember that you will not gain ten pounds from one meal, so take this opportunity to discover how your body feels when you give it what it wants. Is it a pleasant feeling? A satisfying one? Compare this feeling with those you have when you don't eat what you want and are depriving yourself. If you could choose one of those feelings over another, which would it be?

We often forget that our lives are made up of moments and of feelings about moments. As compulsive eaters, we spend our lives forsaking all the moments of satisfaction for a future moment when we will be thin and the deprivation will have paid off. And if and when that moment does come, we are so worried about gaining weight that we focus our attention once more on the future and do not take pleasure in the present.

Most of us miss our own lives. Most of us spend our time preparing for a moment that never comes, while the years slip by, unnoticed, unused.

The means to an end cannot be separated from the end. If you attempt to get thin by reining yourself in, judging yourself, not believing in yourself, you will end up a deprived, self-condemning and frightened human being. And maybe you will have a thin body. For a while.

Breaking free from compulsive eating is also breaking free from preoccupation with the future. It asks, it demands that you be aware of what you are doing *now*. It forces you to examine, by the very questions it asks, the ways in which you rush through your meals – and your days – in perpetual pursuit of moments that may never arrive. It brings up the issues of pleasure and satisfaction and asks that you rediscover their meaning in your life.

If you find that eating what you want is satisfying,

make a mental note of that. Don't create rules like, 'I should always eat what I want'; rather, give yourself permission to eat what you want at least once a day and if it is too frightening, once every few days. Be guided by what feels intuitively right to you (and this you will discover by experience) instead of what you think you should or shouldn't be doing. Eventually you will discover and continue to discover what that is.

If you don't know what you want to eat, you've either let yourself get so hungry you'll eat anything or you're not hungry enough. There's no mistaking the feeling of being ravenous, almost frantic to eat. Try not to let yourself get this hungry because it's both difficult to decide what you want and then to tell when you've had enough. It takes a while for the hunger frenzy to abate and when it does, you've usually eaten past 'enough' and still may not be satisfied because of not eating what you would have wanted had you not been in such a rush.

When you're not hungry enough to eat (but wish you were), some mental images of food may arise, but because they are not connected with physical hunger, it's difficult to choose which to eat. When there's no hunger, there's nothing to satisfy. Wait until the image becomes clear; food will taste better then.

I want a croissant from a bakery in Greenwich Village and I live in Little Rock, Arkansas. Last night, someone in a group said, 'I just can't decide what I want to eat.' Upon further questioning, she discovered she was sabotaging herself by wanting foods in other cities. When she was hungry, she wanted a pastry she had tasted in Paris; not being able to fly there for the night, she'd get discouraged and eat anything she could find. 'What's the use?' she said, if I can't have what I want?'

Eating foods that hum to you is one thing; having to fly 8,000 miles to get them is another. When you find yourself wanting the impossible, it's time to ask yourself what is going on. Kim said, 'I'm afraid that if I let myself eat what I want, I won't eat anything but sweets.' At the bottom of her long-distance fantasies was a fear that if she let herself be realistic and want what was within reach, she'd not only gain weight but be very unhealthy as well. 'Isn't eating sugar all the time terrible for you?' she asked.

Yes. And no. Eating salads and vegetables under restraint and bingeing on sugar whenever you have the chance is not particularly healthy. Feeling deprived is not healthy. Sneaking, hiding, or lying about food is not healthy. Punishing yourself is not healthy.

It's true that eating sugar from morning to night is not a balanced diet, but then again, living in fear of yourself is not a balanced life. Sooner or later you will crave vegetables and protein and when you do, you will eat them because you want them. You will eat them and when you get up from the table, you won't be afraid of what you will do in an hour or tomorrow.

That's what I call healthy.

In each group I hear, 'But how can I eat what I want when I don't know what I want? And if I don't know what I want to eat, how do I know the decisions I make in the other areas of my life are the right ones? How do I ever discover what I want?'

By beginning at the beginning, with where you are right now. If you don't know what you want to eat, it's because you've never given yourself time to explore that and not because you are hopelessly out of touch with yourself. If you don't know what you want to eat, it's because you were never told that what you wanted would be good for you, because you haven't developed trust in your decisions, because you haven't experienced the well-being that comes from giving yourself what you want and watching the self-confidence that grows from such honesty. If you don't know what you want to eat it's because fat is a multi-billion-dollar-a-year industry in our country, and a lot of people stand to lose a lot of money when you start believing that what you want reflects the voice of a self that longs to grow, take good care of itself, satisfy and nurture itself, rather than a self that given choice, would destroy itself.

If you don't know what you want to eat, it's time to find out.

3
Distracted Eating:
It Doesn't Count If
You're Not Sitting Down

'Food tastes better in my mind than on my plate because when I'm just thinking about it, I imagine how delicious it will taste, but when I'm actually eating it, I'm busy thinking about getting the car fixed or watching the evening news.'

A Breaking Free workshop participant

At the end of the first meeting of an eight-week workshop, I give the participants a list of eating guidelines that includes 'eat when you are sitting down.' When I add, 'And that doesn't include the car,' there's a wave of mock groaning and general laughter. I laugh too. I know what it's like to eat in the car. And eat and eat and eat in the car.

My car was favourite restaurant, well-worn kitchen table, and revered dining companion for both my anorexic and subsequent fifty-five pound weight-gain days. I'd go to the store, buy whatever I wanted to eat, and then I would load the passenger seat with my bounty of brown paper bags. When I had a place to go, an appointment to keep, I would eat as much as I could on the way, distract myself while I was there by musing about what I'd eat when I left, and when I was finished I'd hurry back to my car as a lover hurries home to a warm embrace. Food was my hugs, my kisses, my warm embrace. Often I wouldn't have a destination in mind. Often I took rides in my car just to eat.

Eating in my car was safe; no one I knew could see me, question me, judge me. Eating in my car didn't really count. As long as I wasn't sitting at a table, as long as I wasn't eating from a plate, as long as I was moving, having to concentrate on shifting gears, braking, steering, it didn't count. Any food I ate when I wasn't sitting down, either in my kitchen or at a restaurant, didn't count.

You wouldn't believe how much I ate that I didn't eat.

Where you eat and *how* you eat is as important as *what* you eat because it is often upon the first two that you base your recognition *that* you eat.

It doesn't count – you don't really eat – if you eat:

> at the stove cooking, tasting;
> bites off someone else's plate;
> standing in front of the refrigerator/sink;
> ● standing up anywhere;
> ● watching television or a movie;
> reading a book or a newspaper or a magazine;
> when you're involved in an emotional or engrossing or anxiety-producing conversation;
> in the car;
> at someone else's house when no one is around;
> off everyone's dishes when you are cleaning up;
> ● after the meal is over and you didn't eat what you wanted and now you're back (or still) in the kitchen eating what you really wanted;
> ● anywhere at anytime when you feel that you're not allowed or supposed to be eating.

It's not that you're not judging yourself for eating at these times or that your body doesn't get full at these times. It's not really that you eat but don't eat; rather that you eat, but because your attention is focused elsewhere, the food doesn't satisfy you. Or you feel guilty. Or you overeat. And then you eat some more.

We're all familiar with the sense of being somewhere but not *really* being there, the 'sorry, how's that again?' feeling. The need to repeat something or have it repeated because we weren't present. The conversation or event took place, but because our attention wasn't present, it didn't take place for us, in us.

When you're eating and your mind is on something else, you finish but it doesn't seem as if you really ate. But the you that reaches, buys, moves, and puts food in your mouth *did* eat. The you that looks in the mirror, can't fit into clothes, despairs about your body – this you – ate. This is the you that gains weight and no one can understand why because you eat so little at mealtimes.

Here is a list of guidelines designed to focus your attention on eating:

1. Eat in full view of your friends, partner, parents, children, colleagues.
2. Eat when you are sitting down.
3. Eat without distractions – radio, TV, newspapers, books, or loud music.
4. When you eat, do so in as lovely and as nourishing an environment as you possibly can create.
5. When you eat, avoid emotional conversations.

How much do you eat without eating? On a piece of paper, list each of the guidelines. Everytime you eat and follow one of them, put a check next to it. If you followed three of them, put checks next to those three. If you followed all of them, check them all. By the end of a week, it will be visually obvious to you how you distract yourself from tasting, chewing, experiencing satisfaction from eating.

Guideline 1: Eat in Full View of Your Friends, Partner, Parents, Children, Colleagues

When I was in high school, my boyfriend John's mother set a place for me nightly at their dinner table. 'I always have enough food,' she said, 'even if you show up at the last minute because "you eat like a bird."' *I* knew I could polish off half a pizza, a gallon of ice cream, and a box of cookies when I was alone or with my friend Marilyn. I knew I was frantic about food, planned my days according to what I could or couldn't eat. I knew I could eat more than anyone at that table but wouldn't, not only because I was eating in full view of other people but also, and just as important, because it was a meal. It was being served at a table with plates and silverware and napkins.

And I was too fat to eat a meal.

The assumption was that people who are overweight should not be allowed to eat. And if they were, they should eat as little as possible and only of low-caloric foods. The assumption was that people who are overweight and eat real meals are gross. The assumption was that people who are overweight should be spending their time losing weight, not eating, and that sitting down to a meal was tantamount to gaining weight. And, finally, the assumption was that people who are overweight and eat meals are as much as saying they are not ashamed of the way they look and are, in fact, flaunting their fat by eating like someone who doesn't need to lose weight.

If people who are overweight shouldn't eat – *and* we need to eat to live – we must forever pretend that we are not eating when we are eating. When there's no pretending – when we are in full view of others or our attention is focused solely on the food – we must be self-effacing and 'eat like birds.'

When you eat and the majority of your attention is focused on something other than the act of eating, tasting, chewing, satisfying, you are as much as pretending that you are not eating.

Maybe you don't know that you're allowed.

You're allowed.

You're allowed to eat the way you're allowed to breathe and walk and laugh and talk and go to sleep. You're allowed to do these things because you're alive. That's all the qualification you need. If you don't eat, you can't live. Denying your right to eat is, on some level, denying the importance and value of your life. 'Because I am or feel heavier than I think I should or want to be, I don't deserve to dig in and enjoy.' Eating becomes fitful, clandestine. You begin living a lie, eating one way in public and a totally different way when you are alone. 'If they really knew the truth about me, if they knew how much I could eat, if they knew how devouring I am, they would be appalled.' From there, it is a short distance to, 'If they really knew me, they wouldn't love me. Who I am is not worthy of love and must be hidden.' Dishonesty becomes a matter of emotional survival: You must lie, you must hide yourself to be loved. Yet gaining weight is surely not a way of becoming less visible, and the more you hide your eating, the less you hide yourself.

That is such a painful way to live. When you can't tell the truth, you cut the bonds that tie you to other people, bonds of shared emotions like pain and joy and fear and happiness. You start building walls around you instead of bridges between you and others. You start spending more and more time eating, in your car, your bedroom, the bathroom, anywhere you cannot be seen. Then you convince yourself that something is really wrong with you, look at what you are doing, you couldn't possibly tell anyone, no one would understand. So you turn to food. Again. For solace, for comfort. For a warm embrace. And the walls around you become walls of flesh.

More painful than the lies you act out with others are the lies you tell yourself: how much you eat that you don't really eat. The contortions you put yourself through, the extent to which you go, the places you find yourself eating, the humiliation you suffer, to have food.

Marian, a woman in my workshop, says:

> On the way home from work I decided I wanted to binge. I stopped and bought a bag of cookies, ate most of them in my car, and threw the rest of them out of the window. I didn't want to bring them home and have my husband see them.
> The next day I woke up wanting cookies, *those* cookies. So I drove back to the spot where I'd thrown them out. It had rained overnight and the bag of cookies was wet. But I picked them up and sat in my car and ate the rest of the bag of soggy cookies.

Wet cookies don't taste good. Wet cookies are pasty and heavy, and if left sitting on the ground overnight they probably smell, and taste, like dirt. Wet cookies are a little on the disgusting side. No one given the choice between soggy cookies and fresh cookies would choose the former. No one except a person who didn't believe she had a choice. Marian had spent so long hiding and pretending and lying that she could no longer differentiate between what she had to hide from others and what she had to hide from herself that such lying instills: that she is not worthy of enjoying and eating with the grace and dignity that a human being deserves.

When I was living in Big Sur, I was living with a man

I loved who loved me. Still, I spent a lot of time figuring out how, where, and when I could eat without his knowing. There was something about 'getting away with it' that was thrilling and challenging. There was also something about it that was degrading and made me feel like I was going insane. When he'd go to the bathroom, I'd stuff a handful of granola in my mouth. If he left the house for an hour or two, I saw it as 'my chance' to eat. Eating at those times was frenzied and panicked and tasteless. It was an elaborate game, a game in which I got very involved; it was also a game that distanced us because a large part of my emotional life was taking place in secrecy. I unwittingly assigned him the part of myself that judged my food intake and my body size, made rules about what I should and shouldn't eat. When I rebelled by sneaking food and lying to him, I was in effect rebelling and sneaking and lying to myself. The only food for which I was accountable was the food I ate in full view of others. When I gained weight, I was surprised; I had lied to both of us that well.

When you lie, sneak, pretend to others, you lie, sneak, pretend to yourself. When you tell yourself that you are not worthy of eating in full view, you tell yourself that you are not worthy of being seen and known in full view. You send parts of yourself under cover, the vulnerable, frail and most human parts, the parts that reach out and connect with others. You cut yourself off from what you want and need the most: empathy, intimacy, relationship. You cut off the possibility of receiving your warm embrace. Except from a soggy cookie.

For many of us, eating has become akin to stealing. A few months ago I was sitting at a table eating lunch. There were other people around me and I noticed that I felt like I had to rush through my meal, that I still felt as if, by eating, I was doing something wrong.

When I was about six or seven, I stole the record

'Bambi' from our local drugstore. Unfortunately my criminal skills lacked polish: I hid the record under my sweater, its angles sticking out from my chest. To make matters worse, I was with my mother's friend and, as I found out later, she couldn't help but notice what was going on. After dinner my mother sat me down on our brown embroidered couch and told me she knew I had stolen the record and that I would have to go back to the drugstore, return it, and apologize to big ol' bald Harold, the pharmacist, who by now had been apprised of my actions. I was mortified. Apologize? To Harold? Admit that I had stolen 'Bambi'? She must be kidding.

The next day she drove me to the store, waited in the car while I went in, put the record back, walked to the counter, and said, 'My mother says I have to apologize because I stole your record. I'm sorry. Thank you. Good-bye.' And I ran out, ecstatic that it was over. It seemed to my child's mind that the worst part was not that I had done something morally wrong (I liked Bambi. I felt sorry for him – his mother had died) but that I had been caught.

Sometimes when I am eating I feel as if the album cover is sticking out from my chest and that somebody is going to notice and tell me I am doing something wrong and have to apologize. Sometimes when I am eating I worry that I will get caught. I don't know why it is wrong, only that it is, and because I want to avoid the humiliation of apologizing to bald Harold, I'd better sneak or lie, this time with skills that are polished and sophisticated (i.e., having certain areas in my car, apartment, purse where I can stash food and quickly grab for it; learning how to walk and slide food into my mouth at the same time; developing a method of sucking on rather than chewing food so that I can be with some-one and be eating without their knowing).

The elaborate games and rituals we develop to keep us from discovering the truth about ourselves . . . as if the truth was so horrible. The truth about our needs or our fears or our pain.

One afternoon I was alternately talking and crying to my friend Lew about something I had done that I thought was awful. He said, 'You know the things you hate about yourself are the very things I find most interesting, the parts of you that lead you to explore and go deeper and stretch yourself. What you keep trying to hide are the parts of you that will eventually give you wings . . .'

The truths that are never revealed when we sneak and pretend and distract ourselves with food.

Take a piece of paper and:

● Head it with *If —— really knew that I ate or wanted to eat* . . . Then finish the sentence with as many people and as many endings as are true for you. What would happen if your friend Betty or your lover or your mother knew how much you ate and wanted to eat? Would they be afraid to eat with you? Would they think you were less attractive than they do now? Would they still like/love you?

● Head it with *I sneak food because* . . . Why? What would happen if you didn't? Would you get to eat all you want? Would you repulse people by how much you ate? Would they tell you to stop eating if you didn't sneak?

Again, take a few minutes (not a few seconds) to complete the list. Write whatever answers occur to you. Don't think too much about them. Don't censor. Keep writing until no answers arise.

When completed rapidly and honestly, lists can be extremely helpful in uncovering the motivations, decisions, assumptions, and judgements on which your actions and beliefs are based. The value of doing such lists is that when these motivations are revealed, you will no longer be acting on decisions you made before you knew what you know now. You will be able to give yourself a choice about whether you still believe a particular assumption and, if not, what you want to do about it.

For example, if in completing the first list I wrote: 'If Sara really knew what I ate, she'd *look at me more closely and realize why I am so fat,*' my immediate and unconsidered response is that I am fat and that I hide it from Sara by my clothes, posture, and small food intake. The unspoken assumption is that if she knew what I ate, she'd notice that I am fat, and that if she noticed my fat, she wouldn't love me as she loves me now. When I realize that these responses are operating in me and are contributing to feeling uncomfortable and clandestine around Sara and food, I can ask myself if this is actually true: First, am I fat? Second, do I actually believe that I can hide my body from one of my closest friends by eating like a bird when I am with her? And, finally, what difference would it make in my feelings about myself, and Sara's feelings about me, if she knew how much I ate or wanted to eat?

Recently a friend sent a picture she had taken of me when I weighed forty pounds more than I do now. I showed it to Sara. She said, 'Who is that?' I asked her if she were serious. She said, 'Yeah, who is that?'

'That's me Sara. That's me when you first met me. That's me when you first met me and told me I was beautiful.'

'God, Geneen, you looked so different. But I really did think you were beautiful.'

And I remembered how, in those days, I hated my

body and Sara would turn to me and tell me how pretty I was. I remembered that I believed her.

If Sara is so nonjudgemental about my body that she doesn't remember the stages it's been through and the stages it's been through have no effect on her love, then hiding what I eat from her does not agree with reality. My immediate response might reflect an old belief or a past event. Maybe I had a childhood friend who *did* judge me or tease me because of my weight, or maybe I've always been so aware of other people's weight that I think they in turn are passing judgement on mine. Maybe I am so used to sneaking that I find excuses for continuing the habit. Whatever the reasons, they are not, as revealed by my list, what I believe they are. And this discovery allows me the opportunity to rethink my immediate and often unconscious responses. It puts a chink in the heavy metal chain of my belief system. It says 'Wait a minute. You're sneaking because you think she won't love you if you don't. But she does, she has, and barring any major personality changes, she will. You don't *have* to sneak. Do you still *want* to?'

Making lists (or doing whatever reveals our unconscious motivations) sheds light on the forces that move us - forces that were once relevant but have usually outgrown their validity. Becoming aware of the outdated truths on which we base important everyday actions leaves room to establish new truths. It gives us a choice; it enables us to run our own lives instead of being run by them.

If you find that you sneak food consistently, that you lie, pretend, feel undeserving of eating, it probably is for a logical reason. You *aren't* crazy, you *aren't* abnormal. To the extent that you feel compelled to continue and frightened to stop, you are using what you do as a protection, as a way of caring for yourself. Don't try to rip

your behaviour away from yourself – you'll only get
more frightened and feel an even greater need to protect
yourself from what you are frightened of. Move slowly.
Trust that you are providing for yourself, that you
developed these behaviours for good reasons and that
before you can take them away, you must first discover
their purpose. I tell my clients: We're not here not to be
here. If you're doing something that does not make
sense, look deeper. It makes sense.

I began sneaking food when I was about eleven or
twelve. I'd stick two frozen Milky Ways into my pyjama
pants at night and run up the stairs, past my parents'
bedroom. In my room, I'd sit eating them over the round
wooden wastebasket with my back to the door, so that if
my mother walked in I could spit out what was in my
mouth. One night after I had finished them both, I sat on
the floor and sobbed. I was disgusted with myself for eating so many calories. I wanted to be skinny. Weight was
an issue between my mother and me. I wanted her
attention and so I snuck food. I knew that being caught
and gaining weight were guaranteed attention-getters.
Sneaking was also my way of expressing anger at what
I perceived as an unfair condition: having to be thin to
be loved. Sneaking was my way of saying: 'I don't care
what you think or say. I don't care if you love me or not.
I'm going to eat those frozen Milky Ways whether you
like it or not.' Frozen Milky Ways were my mother's –
not my – favourite food.

When I lived in Big Sur, a similar dynamic was
operating. I wanted to assert my independence from
Lee, but I didn't know how to express that independence. I didn't know what kind of work I wanted to do; I
didn't know what to do with my time. I felt lost and confused and needed his attention badly. He was very conscious of my weight because I was always talking about

it. I pushed him away with the food I lied about, pretended I didn't eat. I binged on granola and milk – his favourite breakfast food.

If ever I find myself sneaking food now, I pay close attention to the person from whom I am hiding it and not to how obsessed I feel to be doing this after all these years. I know from past experience that when I sneak, it is an indication that I am not getting something (love, care, attention) I want or need. Sometimes it's an indicator that I feel rejected; sneaking then is my way of saying 'If I can't be myself in front of you, I'll be myself behind your back.'

When I was a child, I didn't have the words, didn't know it was okay to say, 'I'm angry' or 'I need your attention, Mom.' And maybe it *wouldn't* have been okay. Maybe I sensed that my mother was at a particularly vulnerable period in her life (which she was) and felt that if I expressed my anger, she could not have responded with understanding or tolerance. I couldn't afford to alienate my mother; I couldn't pick another. I needed her not only emotionally but for physical survival as well – food, clothing, shelter. Given my understanding of the situation, I pulled myself through the best way I knew how: I swallowed my feelings with frozen Milky Ways.

When I was a child I didn't have a choice; I had one mother. But as a woman I can choose my friends and the people with whom I am intimate, the people I depend upon for understanding and tolerance. There isn't *anyone* I want in my life who is so consistently fragile or intolerant that they cannot sensitively respond to my anger or my need for attention. It's hard enough to say 'I need you' or 'I'm angry'; I don't want friends who turn it against me. I can choose to surround myself with people by whom I feel accepted and heard and valued. And I do.

When you find yourself doing something that doesn't seem to make sense, assume that it does. Then ask yourself what you are trying to do or say by your actions. How is what you are doing helping you? What is it saying for you?

While it might be inappropriate for you to continue sneaking or eating in your car, you need to discover what you are trying to express through that particular action before you can change it. Often the behaviour is triggered by a situation or feeling that evokes an old pain, and in a split second you'll react the way you once did, a way that helped then but which might not be as helpful *now* as other more direct actions. Like using your mouth to speak instead of eat.

Guideline 2:
Eat When You Are Sitting Down

The foods I eat standing up are usually the ones I don't or won't eat sitting down: cake, nibbles, finger food. If I eat chocolate cake when I'm standing, I can rush through it, get it over with, forget that I ate it. Sitting down means deciding to eat. When I eat standing up, I eat without deciding to eat. I eat so fast that I hope I won't notice what I am doing. The result, however, is that I don't feel satisfied.

The act of sitting down signifies that you've acknowledged that you are eating and have decided to give yourself permission to do so. When you give yourself permission, you can slow down, taste the food, decide how much more you want. When you eat and try to do it without getting your own attention, it turns into a race, a challenge: How much can you cram into your mouth before your attention stops you? The answer is: *a lot*.

What kinds of foods do you eat when you are standing?

Are there any specific situations or emotions that trigger eating and standing?

Do you enjoy eating and standing?

For the next week, each time you find yourself standing up while you eat:

● **Sit down.** Wherever you are. If you're in front of the refrigerator, sit down with the door open. If you're standing up at the sink or in front of the TV, sit down. If you're in the office, get a chair. Sit and then notice if there is a change in the way you perceive what you are doing. Notice if there is a change in the drive to eat quickly or before you notice what you are doing.

● **Write it down.** Answer the questions: What was going on before I started eating this? What is it about standing up and eating that I'm enjoying?

Standing at the stove and eating as you cook is another method of eating without really eating. 'I have to taste it before I serve it . . . what if it's too salty?' To a limited extent this reason is valid. But to a greater extent, it is a way of eating a meal and leaving yourself unsatisfied both physically and emotionally. When you eat at the stove, you're not acknowledging your right to sit down at the table. When dinner time finally does arrive, you're full and you eat more and get fuller and more uncomfortable, or you don't eat and wind up feeling you've been cheated out of something special.

Instead you can:

1. Have someone else do the tasting.
2. Limit your tastes to minilicks, bites, teaspoonsful.

Whatever you do, notice how it feels to stand at the stove and eat. Notice whether you enjoy it more than you enjoy sitting down for a meal. Notice whether you do it because you get to eat more that way. Does eating at the stove express a belief about who eats at the stove and when? Did your mother eat at the stove or did she sit down and eat with the family? Are you doing what you think you should do, have always done, or is it what you want to do?

Guideline 3: Eat Without Distractions – Radio, TV, Newspapers, Books, or Loud Music

When I mention this guideline to a group, I get glares, frowns, stunned expressions. Silence. Then: 'I can't do that'; 'That's absurd'; 'If I can't read the *New Yorker* cartoons, I can't enjoy the food'; 'Ann Landers helps my digestion'; 'I should have listened to my husband. He told me not to come'; 'Tom Selleck makes me eat less.'

Yes. We've got a lot invested in distracting ourselves when we eat. It's very hard to eat when we eat. (It's very hard to do *anything* and not be distracted.) And we like eating. But how much can we like it when we're forever concentrating on something else while we do it?

If distracting yourself reflects an underlying belief that it is indulgent and greedy to allow yourself the time to eat without working or reading, then you are probably overeating on a consistent basis; overeating to make up for or rebel against the fact that you won't allow yourself the right to eat at all.

Eating and reading, eating and watching TV, eating and focusing your attention on anything or everything else aside from the food are less blatant indicators than sneaking, but they are still ways of pretending, of getting the food into you without having to take responsibility for, and be aware of, what you are doing. You can easily overeat in these circumstances, because you aren't fully tasting the food or focused on the subtle sensations of satisfaction. You can eat and go unconscious. Which is fine – and I mean that – if that's what you want to do. At certain moments, I consciously decide to be unconscious. I'm tired of being aware and taking responsibility for my actions . . . I want a break. And I take it. I stand at the sink and eat a pretzel. I read a book and eat spaghetti. But my heart isn't pounding at those times. I don't feel that I'm doing something wrong and that if someone walked in, I'd have to hide the food under my bed.

If you are adamant about not giving up reading or watching TV or working while you eat, notice that. Notice the vehemence behind your feeling. Make room for that vehemence; don't try to push it away. Instead, during a meal in which you are distracting yourself, gently become aware of how much you taste the food, how tuned in you are to your body while you are eating, and what is enjoyable to you about the meal.

For one meal – only one – decide that you won't watch TV or read or work. Watch what happens.

If you find it uncomfortable, ask yourself why. Is it because you feel you don't deserve to be spending all your attention on food? Are you thinking about the time you're wasting and all the things you should be doing instead?

If the answer to these questions is yes, eat one meal a day for four or five days without distractions. Does it become easier? If it does, try eating two meals a day without distractions. If it doesn't get any easier after a few days, try it for another few days. If a meal is too long a time, try focused eating with a snack. Pay careful attention to the feelings that come up, without judging them. Just notice.

Is it hard because it's a habit or a ritual and habits and rituals are difficult to break?

Is it hard because you're emulating a family member or cherished friend and doing what they do makes you feel closer to them?

Ask yourself if it really works for you to eat with distractions. Be honest.

Guideline 4: When You Eat, Do So in as Lovely and as Nourishing an Environment as You Possibly Can Create

When you have a guest for dinner, you probably take the time or trouble to set the table, light some candles, use pretty linen or flatware or place settings. You want it to be just right. Your guest is special.

So are you.

Take the time for yourself that you would spend on someone else. Someone you really like.

It sounds attractive but it isn't easy. When you live alone, you say. 'It's too much bother for one person,' and when you don't live alone, 'It's too much bother. Period.'

Blazing new patterns requires effort and persistence. It's much easier to fall into old habits than to take the time to establish new ones. But once they're established, they're established. And then they replace and become as constant as the old ones.

You *are* special. And the whole experience of a meal changes when you give yourself the message that you deserve this kind of attention. You sit down to eat as a person who is not doing anything wrong by eating. You are sitting down as a person who is allowed and expected to eat.

Guideline 5: When You Eat, Avoid Emotional Conversations

When I'm angry or sad, my stomach contracts and my throat gets tight.

When I'm happy or excited, my heart quickens and my stomach contracts.

I am thirty-three. For seventeen years I ate when I was happy, ate when I was sad, ate when I was excited. For seventeen years my response to every emotion was to eat. It wasn't until five years ago that I realized that eating when I was caught up in an emotion was like pouring water into an already overflowing glass. There was no room for it.

When your mind and body are involved in reacting, eating is inappropriate. Food cannot be used at that time. Digestion slows while other physiological mechanisms go into play: the heart beats faster, adrenalin is released, strength is increased. Your body is protecting itself, getting ready for whatever comes next.

When you're involved in an emotional or tense conversation while you eat, you eat the feelings along with the food. You swallow the anxiety, the clutched nerves, the troubled feelings, and what you are left with is a body that is anxious, clutched, troubled, and, now, full. Ice cream does not melt the lumps in your throat.

If you're meeting a friend or a business colleague for a meal, try to avoid highly charged conversation until after you've eaten. Or meet them for tea or a walk. Or meet them and don't do anything but talk. That's enough.

For many people, this is an arcane guideline. 'What do you *mean* we eat feelings?' The idea of cutting out business lunches or dinner meetings with lovers or friends or colleagues to discuss work or go over an argument or talk about a new idea seems unnecessary.

But the idea whenever possible is to eat when you eat and work when you work and be sad when you're sad. And to watch what happens when you don't.

The idea is not to force yourself to do anything or judge yourself for what you already do. The idea is to see what works toward the ultimate idea: eating that is not urgent or frenetic or guilt-ridden.

In the end, you must discover what works for *you*. Don't use these guidelines as rules or as truth. Question my suggestions – try them and see if they help you feel better about yourself. If they don't, do something that does. The idea is to improve the quality of your life, not to make you miserable about failing at yet another weight-related programme.

4
Knowing When to Stop Eating: When Enough Is Enough

'If one is good, more is better.'

My mother

Twice a year our family visited my grandparents in Texas. We looked forward to my grandmother's cooking for weeks, knowing that soon after we got there we'd be at a table resplendent with blintzes, borscht, brioches, schnecken, and coffeecake. Each of us had our own system of eating: My mother concentrated on borscht and blintzes, my brother piled his plate with one of everything; I took one item at a time, saving the best, the blintzes, for last. When we were so full we pushed our chairs back from the table, my grandmother said, 'Now, eat one more than enough. Then you'll be satisfied.' She said this every year at the end of every meal for as long as I can remember. And I still don't know what she meant.

One more what? One more bite? Slice? Spoonful? Bowl?

What was enough? I seemed to go from hungry to full to too full to nauseated.

Did enough mean satisfied? Or did it mean full?

These are the questions that I hear many times during each workshop. The first step in breaking free is letting yourself eat when you are hungry. The next step is learning what you are hungry for, and eating it. After that, you learn when enough is enough. And whereas hunger can be insistent and loud and unmistakable, enough can be subtle and quiet and easy to miss.

My friend Janice has a lover for the first time in three years. A few days ago she told me, 'I don't know when to stop making love. It's been so long that even after hours of lovemaking, even when I'm exhausted and all I want to do is close my eyes and go to sleep, I want to make love.'

Even now that Janice is physically intimate with a lover, she is still in pain about the years she wasn't. Part of her is still crying herself to sleep alone; she hasn't caught up with herself. She's living in the past and the future both: aching for what she didn't have and trying to store up for what she might not have again.

Deprivation and insatiability go hand in hand. When you feel you're not allowed to have it, and are eating it anyway, you don't want to give up what might be your only chance at eating it. When you feel you're not allowed to have it, you are focused on getting as much of it as you can. Satisfaction is irrelevant. Enough at these times is being physically incapable of one more swallow.

When you stop eating depends on *why* you are eating and how you want to feel when you get done.

After the first few weeks of a workshop, or working by yourself on your eating patterns, it becomes easy to recognize hunger. Hunger rumbles and groans. Too much of it makes you irritable and edgy, sometimes frantic. It is at this point that workshop participants begin saying, 'So now I'm eating when I'm hungry, but once I start I can't seem to stop myself until all the food is gone and I'm stuffed. Now what?'

These are the 'now what's':

Be very sure that you are hungry before you begin eating. If you aren't, you will have no physical trigger, short of being very full, to tell you to stop eating because you had no physical trigger that told you to start. If you eat when you aren't hungry, chances are that you will consistently overeat. Your body is receiving something it didn't ask for and doesn't need at that time. Like trying to nap when you're not tired, it doesn't fit.

There's *nothing wrong* with eating when you're not hungry. Sometimes after a hard day you walk in the door and you want nothing – not a hug or a kiss or a long-awaited letter or a call from a friend – but food. You're not being bad, you are using food to soothe non-physical hungers. Be as specific as you can about what you want to eat and then, as I tell my clients, sit down, and eat. But don't expect your body to tell you, before you're full, to stop. It didn't tell you to start, and that's not why you are eating. Forget the guidelines. Allow yourself to eat for the warmth or the texture or the activity of it, and when whatever it was in you that needed food has had enough, you'll stop. That may be after a few bites and may not be until your pants are unbuttoned and all you want to do is sleep. Tomorrow, Scarlett, is another day.

Satisfaction is relative to your moods, your emotional needs, your physiological well-being. What satisfies you one day may not be enough the next day. Most of the time I like stopping when I still have room for more food. I enjoy the feeling of lightness, the feeling of not being hungry but not being full.

Not long ago I was in a car accident, a near head-on collision in which the driver's side of my car was smashed by another car at fifty-five miles per hour. I emerged unscratched but very shaken and with a strong sense of my human fragility. Immediately after the accident, I wanted to be touched. I wanted something next to me that was alive, a breathing, beating, warm-flesh body. Living alone and unable to get that kind of sustained physical intimacy, I fell asleep crying. The next day I noticed that when I got hungry I wanted large, heavy, hot meals: rice and vegetables, baked potatoes, lasagne and bread, eggs and toast. I wanted to be full. I wanted to be warm. I wanted to feel the solidity and strength of my body. I was so glad to be alive, and I was turning to the next best thing I knew after a person: food. So I watched myself eat three big meals a day instead of my regular two, and I figured that my body was adapting to the accident and knew what it needed. In the back of my mind was the by-now familiar voice: 'Oh my God. I can't believe you are eating so much. You'll be a blimp if this continues. How about a carrot for dinner?'

It is possible that had I been touched and cuddled and held I would not have wanted so much food. But I doubt it. I would have still been walking around with the feeling of fragility, the overwhelming fear that my body could shatter at any moment. I would still have wanted to feel full and warm and solid. But even if I was turning to food *only* because I couldn't turn to a person, that's good enough. The crux of living is not to be thin at any cost. We hope we can give ourselves the support and nourishment and warmth we need as freely and lovingly as possible. When that resource is food, we can let ourselves eat. *With awareness*. Because without that awareness we are back at the beginning: eating from sadness or loneliness or fear, eating because we're happy or excited or glad, eating because nothing tastes as good as food. Eating mindlessly, eating thoughtlessly, eating because there's nothing better to do.

Sometimes our predominant need may be to feel light, not only because we like the way we look, but because feeling light fits in with the way we are living our lives. We may be moving, dancing, travelling; it may be the time of year when we feel most energetic and creative, and eating heavy meals pulls on our energy, drags us down. Then, we can eat accordingly. But *needs change* from day to day, season to season and, with them, what satisfies us also changes.

When you live a life based on the externally imposed and inflexible need to be thin, it is impossible to develop trust in your ability to eat what satisfies you because what you are believing is that *being thin* will satisfy you. Being thin when you're not thin is just an idea, and ideas don't keep you warm. When you *are* thin and need to be touched, you are thin and need to be touched. Being thin does not take away the realization that you almost died in a head-on collision. Being thin cannot touch you or hold you.

We forget that our lives are made up of continual unfoldings that ideally take us closer and closer to balance and clarity. We forget, in believing that being thin will satisfy us, that the issue is not thinness but satisfaction. What if our thinking, influenced by advertising, media, and cultural expectation, has been turned around and, in fact, we don't *know* what will satisfy us? What if we begin with the awareness that what we want is satisfaction and try to discover what will bring us closer to it, instead of thinking we already know and working backward?

Satisfaction is as psychological as it is physical. The mind and body are so closely intertwined that how you feel emotionally – the ups and downs, little joys and sorrows of a day – affects how you feel physically. How you feel will determine what and how much you eat, and what and how much you eat will in turn determine how you feel.

When you are about to eat, ask yourself if you are hungry. Be honest with yourself. (If the answer is no, that doesn't mean that you can't eat.) Then ask yourself what you would choose right this second if you could have anything at all. Would it be to stop working and take the rest of the day or night off? Would it be a walk, a bath, a kiss? A new outfit? A lover, a house, a car? If it's anything other than food, you will probably eat until you are overstuffed because you're settling, and settling does not lend itself to satisfaction. It may not be possible to have a new house or car or lover, but it *is* possible not to add to your dissatisfaction. When you want a new car and you admit to yourself that you want it, an ice cream sundae won't do.

If after asking yourself what you truly want when you are not hungry and are about to eat, the answer is food, ask again. Play with yourself. Say, 'Are you sure that food is what you want?' If, after a few times, the answer consistently comes back, 'Yes, I want food and I want it now. Gimme,' give yourself some food. But with an open heart and not with the feeling that you're doing something wrong. Because as soon as you're not allowed, you want it more. And then it becomes impossible to be clear about what you are attempting to satisfy: the rebellious child in you who feels wronged and wants to do the opposite of what she's told or the empty or sad or angry or lonely adult who wants to take care of herself by eating.

Eat and be done with it. *Everyone* eats compulsively. Everyone eats sometime during their lives because food is available and it tastes good and they don't know what else to do or how to deal with their feelings. The difference between them and you is that they don't punish themselves for hours or days afterwards. They eat and then they go on to the next thing. You can do that too.

Pay close attention to what feels like 'enough' to you over a period of a few weeks. Each time you eat, rate yourself on a hunger scale of 1 to 10. And when you finish eating, rate yourself again. Five is comfortable, below 5 is increasingly empty, and above 5 is increasingly full. Notice how you feel about yourself when you stop at 6 or above.

Do you *like* the feeling of being full?

Does it give you a sense of solidity and groundedness?

On a day – and only for one meal – on which you are not feeling particularly needy or unhappy, try eating until 4 on the scale. How does that feel to you? Give yourself a few hours to discover how that lightness affects the rest of your thoughts, feelings, interactions.

Begin some kind of movement – walk, dance, venture up some stairs – and notice if and how feeling light affects your body. Do that same movement when you have eaten at 6 or above; notice the difference. Which way is more comfortable? Try it a second time with another meal. Pay close attention to your reactions.

Every time you *choose* to stop when you could continue you are acting from a desire to care for yourself, you are acting without compulsion. You are breaking free.

Listen for the small quiet voice that says 'I've had enough.' The difference between hunger and enoughness can be, and often is, a bite or maybe two. If you are quiet enough and not directing your attention elsewhere you can hear the bodily transition to satisfaction. When you have had enough it's as if a door latches, something clicks. Your body is saying 'I've had enough.

You can keep eating if you want but I'm ready to stop.' That voice is quiet and easy to miss, especially when you aren't used to hearing it or when the food tastes so good you don't want to hear it.

In workshops, people often say, 'I don't have that voice. It's just not there.' I don't believe that. I think it takes time and confidence in the basic wisdom of your body to allow that voice expression. Many theories contradict its validity, among which the most popular are: It takes twenty minutes for your brain to register the amount of food you've eaten and therefore to signal you that you are full; your stomach is stretched by years of overeating and cannot be relied on to regulate itself. But it always gets down to what you believe. Believing in either of those two theories and eating accordingly doesn't give you a lot of control. They are beliefs that render you, at the moment you are eating, powerless. How do you decide when you've had enough if your stomach is so stretched it doesn't recognize satisfaction?

When you're in the middle of a meal and it tastes so good that all you can think about is how good it tastes and you don't want to stop, don't stop. Eat all you want. And then what? How do you feel? Do you feel satisfied, gross, guilty, disgusted with yourself? If eating had nothing to do with what you looked like and you could eat like this and have exactly the kind of body you wanted, would you keep choosing to eat this amount? Do you feel comfortable? Are you at ease in your body?

When you're in the middle of a meal and it tastes so good that all you can think about is how good it tastes and you don't want to stop . . . stop. The hand-to-mouth movement is mesmerizing – it's as if the world stops while you're eating, which, appealing as that notion may be, is exactly why it's helpful to pause mid-way in a meal: to remind yourself that your plate or the kitchen counter or the refrigerator is not the heartbeat of the earth and that if you stop eating you really will find other places to put yourself, other things to do.

When you're eating and have gotten caught in the hand-to-mouth movement, be conscious that you are unconscious. That's all it takes. That's a big 'all it takes,' but on the other hand, it's not complicated or esoteric. You can break the spell by becoming aware of your body, other objects in the room. Breathe deeply. Raise your eyes from the food. Focus on something, anything.

If you are with other people, put your fork or spoon down and get involved in what's happening around you: the conversation, the activity, the decor. Then ask your-self how you feel: Are you still hungry, does your body (not your mind) want more food? If you were driving in your car at that moment would you feel you needed food – or do you want to eat because it's in front of you? If you don't know if you are satisfied, take two or three more bites. Then pause again. What does your body say now? If you're not full, not hungry, but don't know if you're satisfied, stop eating for five minutes. Tell yourself you can continue if you want to, but for now you are going to stop.

Many factors contribute to the pull that food exerts on us and to the difficulty we have in stopping the hand-to-mouth movement. Among these are:

● **'The clean-the-plate club.'** It comes in different guises: 'Clean your plate and you can have dessert'; 'Clean your plate and you can watch television.' The message is: 'When you clean your plate you are entitled to do what you want to do.' Or, conversely: 'When you don't clean your plate you will be punished.' Underlying this childhood bribery is the unspoken message that your body is not to be valued as a reliable source of information. The message is: Your body – its likes, dislikes, satisfaction levels – cannot be trusted; someone else knows better than you what and how much you should eat.

Thirty years later, the clean-the-plate club members are still cleaning their plates, eating more than their bodies need, feeling judgemental about their bodies, and wondering why it's so hard to get up from the table when there's food left on their plates.

When anything, including food, is used for bribery, benign as it may seem, that object thereafter becomes charged with meaning, i.e., it isn't just food anymore: Thinking about it and pushing it away is significant on the psychological as well as the physical level. Food thereafter is imbued with the consequences of listening to intuitive versus authoritative messages.

If you grew up with the clean-the-plate injunction and still find it difficult to leave food on your plate, you are probably still operating on unwritten messages and assumptions communicated to you in childhood. To stop cleaning your plate, you need to recognize exactly what those assumptions are. Spend some time thinking back on family scenes when cleaning your plate was an issue: Do you remember any specific feelings you had about yourself during these times? What kind of bribes were made? Did you feel that by cleaning your plate you would be pleasing someone you wanted to please, someone whose love you felt you needed? What happened when you didn't clean your plate?

● **'The children in India are starving, so eat your dinner.'** I used to think that meant my piece of meat would transport itself to India if I didn't eat it, so I'd better hurry up before it grew wings. A variation on this theme is, 'When I was a child (during the Depression or living in poverty) we would have given anything to have this food . . . so be grateful and eat.'

It's true that hunger is a worldwide problem, and alleviating it is a worthy endeavour. It is also true that some of our parents grew up hungry and poor, which must have been very painful. But eating beyond comfort and desirability will not alleviate either one of those problems. Ever. It won't even increase your empathy or political consciousness. All it *will* do is help you gain weight.

A friend of mine has a cartoon on her refrigerator: A Chinese woman is talking to a small boy who is sitting at a table before a bowl of rice. She's saying, 'Eat your rice. Think of all the children in America eating nothing but junk food.'

● **Leaving food on your plate.** I recently had a first date with a man who, at dinner, finished his very large salad (with croutons and cheese and garbanzo beans and pasta), baked potato (with sour cream, chives, butter, and bacon), a large bowl of turkey soup, and a glass of beer, then reached across the table to my half-eaten salad, soup, and baked potato and began systematically polishing them off. After he had disposed of my salad and was starting on my baked potato, I asked if he were still hungry. 'Nope,' was the answer.

'Is there any reason why you're eating everything that isn't eating you first?'

'I can't stand wasting food,' he said with a glare. 'I can't stand waste of any kind.'

I could have let the first objection go, the one about wasting food. But not the second, the one with the hint

of self-righteousness and political correctness. Here's
how our conversation went:

ME: How are you defining 'waste'?

HE: Oh, you know, anything that's squandered or
misused. Anything left over that really could
be used.

ME: Used by whom?

HE: By the person who's leaving it over.

ME: Even if, in the case of food, that person has had
enough?

HE: What's having enough? Don't you think that's
a little whimsical? You eat till you finish
what's on your plate. Then you don't waste
food.

ME: What if there's food left over in the serving
bowl? Do you eat that too?

HE: Not if I'm full.

ME: Waste is what's left over on the plate but not
in the serving bowl?

HE: Yes.

ME: Isn't *that* a little whimsical or, more to the
point, ridiculously arbitrary? At what point
do you decide not to finish it all? What if you're
in a restaurant and they couldn't fit the entire
portion on your plate? Do you ask the waiter if
there's food left in the kitchen because, after
all, if there was you'd be wasting it?

HE: I think you're carrying this a little too far. I'm
talking about not wasting what *I am in
control of*.

ME: That's just the point: You are often *not* in
control of the size of your portions or how
hungry or full you are at a given point. But

you *are* in control of what you put in your body and therefore how you feel afterward.

HE: Yeah, so what I'm saying is that when I'm in control of what I put in my body I want to finish what's on my plate. And that I feel better when I do.

ME: And what I'm saying is that if you're at a restaurant or someone's home, the portions you receive may not be synchronous with your hunger. When you finish all your food all the time without regard to your body, which is, after all, what you are feeding, that's compulsive. Compulsive is when you are driven to do something that is out of touch with the present situation. You give up choice. And then you relinquish responsibility for your weight because when you eat more than your body needs, it's like squandering, it turns the food to fat. Fat is excess. And isn't that, according to your definition, waste?

He told me he was sorry he ever mentioned it, pleaded with me to stop talking so that he could compulsively eat in peace, and said he would never again make the mistake of tossing up food-related comments for dinner-time chatter. 'Chatter,' I blinked at him hard. 'This isn't chatter,' I thought, 'and unless you take your foot out of your mouth there won't be any room there for *my* potato.'

Everyone has his or her own definition of what's wasteful. It seems to me that loading a body with food it doesn't need is the same as throwing it away, and just as wasteful.

Once we acknowledge the subjectivity of our definitions of waste and the conditioning upon which they're based, we are in a position to make a choice about how we want to act now. For people who have been deeply affected by poverty or scarcity of food, this may take some time, and not everyone wants to or feels the need to change their habits. If not wasting food is not an obstacle in their lives, there is not sufficient impetus to do the work of bringing deeply woven responses to the surface. You need to decide for yourself what's important enough for you to spend your time on.

Let's say you have acknowledged your beliefs about waste. You've thought about them, written about them, talked about them, and redefined them. Then you go out to dinner and start a delightful meal. Halfway through, you realize you've had enough. But it tastes so good. You look down at your plate. You think of the starving children in India, how criminal it would be to waste this food. You might as well eat it. Then you remember that you're not doing that anymore, that this food will never get to India. But it still looks good. And the taste of it . . . you want some more. You've reached the critical moment. Here are some suggestions to live through it:

● **Push your plate away.** Move it to the side. Ask the waiter to take it away. When you're not looking at it any longer, your mind will focus on something else. If you're at home, either push your plate away or get up and put it on the kitchen counter. Much compulsive eating occurs because the food is in front of you and you keep your hands busy by picking at it. When it's not there, you can't pick.

● **If you're in a restaurant, ask for a 'doggie bag.'** Bring the food home. If you want it, eat it tomorrow. If not, give it to the dog. Or cook something original and throw the leftovers in.

● **If you're at home, wrap up the food and put it away.** Do whatever you want with it tomorrow: eat it, give it away, cook it again.

● **Throw the food away.** Whenever I bring this up in group there is an uproar of dissenting opinions. Everyone's got her own particular morality and extremely convincing justifications to sustain it.

I suggest that you try throwing some food away three times. The first two times may be too emotionally loaded for you to feel anything but frightened. But on the third try, you may notice that when you throw it away, you have a feeling of being in control rather than of being controlled. There's nothing that deglamorizes food more than throwing it down the toilet or mushing it in the garbage with cold coffee grounds.

● **Decide beforehand that for a period of a few days or a week you are going to leave a few bites of food on your plate at each meal.** This is easy to decide beforehand and easy not to do at the moment. Make a commitment to it. Decide that you want to know what it's like to consistently be comfortable with your food intake, to feel powerful and in charge of your eating. Go slowly. Make the commitment for one meal, then the next. It's not always going to be easy. But you can get through the hard moments by reminding yourself that (1) you can eat anytime you get hungry and that (2) you are taking care of yourself even though it may not seem like it at the moment. Ask yourself how you want to feel when you get *done* eating. Allow yourself that much tenderness.

● **Beware of the rationalization, 'This is my last or only chance to have this food. I should eat it while I can get it.'**

It usually is not true. You can ask for the recipe or you can go out and get it or something similar tomorrow when you are hungry.

When it is true, eating it when you are not hungry doesn't change that. It might very well be your only chance to eat a particular meal (i.e., if you are in a foreign country or travelling somewhere away from home), but the fact remains that when you're not hungry and you keep eating, the taste of food becomes secondary. You're trying to feed the *feeling* of deprivation and scarcity, the fear of not getting enough. The same panic provokes bingeing: 'I'm going to diet tomorrow; I won't be able to have it anymore so I'd better eat all I can now.' The feeling that there *just is not enough to go around.* Storing up, packing it in for the nameless moment in the future when all of everything good will be gone and you'll be left barren and aching and hungry.

You cannot store sensation. If you eat the whole thing now, you might still wake up in two days wanting to eat it again and it won't be there. We try to override the pain of wanting and not having by making ourselves so sick when we do have that we never have to go through the pain of wanting it again. If this is our last chance to eat ice cream for years and we eat a quart or more tonight and get utterly sickened by not only the taste but just the mention of ice cream, we might not want it for a year.

You cannot feed a feeling with food. The fear of never getting enough does not go away when you eat everything on your plate because you might not get it again.

You might not get it again. But you absolutely *will* eat again. And you will eat delicious, exotic, luscious food again. Every country, city, family has culinary wonders. It's *never* your last chance to have something good.

I find it peculiar and poignant that we try to make good things, feelings, tastes go on for ever and ever. On a cultural and personal level, we try to extend a youthful appearance and deny the importance of old age and death – as if there were anything that lasted forever.

When I first began going out with boys, I'd spend endless hours fantasizing about my Saturday night date. For days I'd plan what I was going to wear, say, do that night; dream about how he would kiss me and how I would or wouldn't push him away. I'd imagine myself married to him, having children with him, going to South America with him, riding on elephants and planes with him. Then Saturday would come. And I'd spend the whole day preparing: washing my hair, laying out my clothes, getting dressed, putting on make-up. Then Saturday night would come. Then Sunday. And it would be over. And I couldn't believe it was over. All those days of dreaming, planning, fantasizing, all those days when I wanted Saturday to come so badly but didn't ever consider that Sunday would follow. And then it was Sunday. And I didn't know what to do with all that letdown. It didn't seem fair. How could it be over so quickly? I wanted it back. But more than wanting Saturday, I wanted the days of excitement before Saturday. I wanted something to look forward to. Without the edge of anticipation and waiting, life seemed dull and meaningless. So I'd find another person or event to build my life around, replace my hopes on. I lived those years waiting for Saturdays, waiting for a moment I never wanted to come because then it would be over.

The worst part about eating is that it's over so soon. You look forward to it, you plan your day around it, and then it's over. And you don't want it to be over. Because it's a high point, because you have to go on to the next thing. And you might not want to go on to the next thing. It might not be as instantly gratifying as food. It might not be gratifying at all.

But prolonging a meal does not stop it from ending. Sooner or later you have to get up from the table and go on to the next thing. And your choice is whether you go on to the next thing feeling comfortable and satisfied or miserable and stuffed.

On the bright side, you will get hungry again. You will have the chance to look forward to eating and to actually eating again. When you can allow the meal to end, you make way for another meal to begin, one that may be even better than the last.

If the worst part about eating is that it's over so soon, the best thing about eating is that the sooner it's over, the sooner you get to do it again.

Pay close attention to the point at which your focus moves from how good the food tastes to the urgency or desire to eat all you can while you can. The shift usually occurs after you've had enough and before all the food is gone. Notice the change in the quality of your eating, the messages you give yourself. Notice if there is a shift in your self-image from feeling secure and glad to be eating so well to fears about getting enough.

Notice what part the food plays in this unfolding. For instance, are you still tasting it? Are you still enjoying it?

If you were told you could have food again anytime you wanted it, would you still be eating it?

At what point are you willing to stop eating and say, 'I want to feel good. I want to take care of myself. I do not want to get up from this table feeling stuffed and miserable and unable to concentrate'?

At every meal you have the chance to care for yourself or cause yourself discomfort. The choice is yours.

5
Bingeing: When Enough Isn't Enough

'I'd like to order the idea of five desserts, please.'

A friend to a waitress

This chapter is about what to do when you find yourself knee-deep in food, frantic and wanting to stop more than anything in the world but not wanting to stop more. It is also about what you can do to prevent that from happening and what you can do after it's happened.

Bingeing does not necessarily mean standing in front of the refrigerator with one hand in a pot of vegetables, the other hand in a box of cookies, while the cold pizza and last night's meat loaf wait their turn in your mouth. Bingeing is an attitude; bingeing is qualitative. As with any symptom, the root causes must be acknowledged and, to some extent, dealt with before the symptom will disappear. Bingeing is not only the act of eating and its concomitant feelings but all the moments, decisions, and feelings that lead up to that act. Bingeing is a symptom. Once it happens it becomes a problem in itself, but it is foremost a symptom – a symptom that decisions, feelings, and attitudes about yourself, your relationships, and food that preceded the onset of the binge are not serving you. Bingeing is only the tip of the iceberg.

In *Feeding the Hungry Heart*, I wrote that 'Binges are purposeful acts, not demented feelings . . . a binge can

. . . be an urgent attempt to care for yourself when you feel uncared for. Binges speak the voice of survival. They are . . . signals that something is terribly wrong, that you are not giving yourself what you need – either physically (with food) or emotionally (with intimacy, work, relationships). They are your last stand against deprivation.'

Binges are marked by urgency, by the feeling of 'I want it and I want it now.' The feeling of 'I want it now so badly that I will run down anything standing in my way.' Binges are marked by the temporary suspension of belief in anything other than food. A binge is a plunge into oblivion. A binge is a dry drunk. When I used to drink a lot, it took four or five glasses of wine to blur the world. Now it takes one. When I used to eat a lot it took an hour of nonstop eating and the resulting discomfort for me to classify the act as a binge. Now it takes my awareness of the urgency with which I need food – any food and any quantity of food – for me to classify the act as a binge. Two cookies can be a binge.

We all need plunges into oblivion. Sometimes living is too much to handle. Sometimes I'll find myself, who doesn't like the taste of liquor, saying 'I need a drink' when what I am really saying is 'I need to tune out, pull in the antennae, and do nothing, absolutely nothing, for half an hour. Not have to be responsible to my friends, not have to listen to anyone's troubles with food, not have to write. I need to stop being a disciplined, responsible, working adult, author, group leader, friend, lover, daughter and let the world take care of itself while I take care of myself.'

That's when I take myself into the living room, sprawl out on the floor, and lie there for half an hour. That's when I notice that the poplar trees outside my window have lost their leaves. That's when the need to binge can drop away.

We can excuse ourselves for doing nothing when we eat because eating is doing something. No one will know by walking in the room whether we're eating because we're hungry or eating because we need to get off the carousel and this is the only stop. Eating is a socially acceptable way of taking time for ourselves. All else is defined as indulgence. Or selfish or unnecessary or a waste of time.

We all need plunges into oblivion.

Step one in preventive bingeing is to find what, for you, constitutes a plunge into oblivion that is not food or drink. And to do it once a day for fifteen minutes.

Every time I mention this in a group, the participants immediately want to know what my oblivions are. After I stammer, blush, and ask them why they want to know (you can tell if it's a true oblivion because you won't want anyone to know about it. True oblivions don't mesh with the image you want to project and are definitely not politically correct), I tell them. So, for the record, my oblivions are: 'All My Children,' *People* magazine, buying legwarmers that glitter, jasmine bubble baths, my living room floor, and my current fantasy that a departed lover who was unprepared to make a commitment will return to my door with flowers and a tattoo on his chest that says 'forever yours.'

The most common complaint I hear in the groups is, 'But there's nothing that's as good as eating.' And to some extent this is true. Nothing *tastes* as good as eating. But because it's not acceptable in our culture to 'waste time,' other things we might like to do are uncontested in the competition with food for oblivion. The reason so many of us turn to food when we need relief or escape is that we don't know we're permitted to do otherwise. Everyone *has* to eat; we need food to live. But we don't need bubble baths, soap operas, or *People* magazine. Our work ethic admonishes us to spend our time doing only what is productive and necessary. And we obey.

My friend Barbara says, 'What our culture defines as indulgence I think is necessary. And what it thinks is necessary I think is irrelevant.'

Bingeing as a 'last stand against deprivation' is the voice of a self that will not tolerate, not for another minute, the denial of all that *it* thinks is necessary and that *you* think is indulgent. And rather than acknowledge that what is needed is unstinting, openhanded, and self-directed generosity, many people attempt to counter their bingeing with more and more dietary restrictions, and in so doing tighten the noose around a self that is already starving for attention.

In order to change anything, and this belief is no exception, you must first understand how what you now believe affects your actions. You cannot change anything you don't even know you believe. Naming what you already believe and are acting upon is the prerequisite of change. Finding this belief is not especially difficult – it requires honesty and patience – but it is daring because in many instances, it means being willing to challenge beliefs you value and accept as the truth.

Let's look at three culturally pervasive and media-reinforced beliefs about bingeing:

1. You binge because you lack will power, determination, and discipline.
2. Taking time for yourself is indulgent and self-ish.

3. To stop bingeing, you must clamp down on yourself and, from somewhere in your psyche, create more will power, determination, and discipline.

Each of these beliefs catalyses the following set of actions that is confluent with the belief:

1. When you binge, you start feeling bad about yourself – it shows character flaws. *What's the matter with you? Where is your will power? Are you going to be spineless for the rest of your life?*
2. In an effort not to be, or appear to be, indulgent or selfish, you busy yourself with doing more and more things for others, especially if you feel or are overweight. *Fat people don't deserve pleasure . . . Look at their bodies . . . They've already indulged themselves to the utmost . . .* Your time is consumed in doing, going, being available. Although you feel dry and rocky inside, you keep going, doing, being.
3. Frantic about your bingeing and the pounds you're gaining, you decide you'll diet. Tomorrow. You decide to cut more and more pleasure-giving foods from your daily intake. Because of the judgement about your weight, your body and your spinelessness – you don't go gently with yourself – you won't buy clothes that fit, you won't socialize, you won't let yourself in. You won't like yourself. You won't. You won't. You won't.
You won't treat yourself with the respect that you would expect from a stranger.

The idea that bingeing is a sign that you need to give yourself more and not less (food, attention, etc.) contradicts the widely accepted belief that bingeing is self-indulgent. When, after a binge, you have the courage to 'indulge yourself' by providing pleasures for yourself that aren't culturally accepted, you are perceived as a threat to the established norm. When you make yourself different from those around you, when you say, 'I need time for myself; I'm not going here and I won't do that for you today; and I know you need this but right now I am taking a bath,' people stop and stare. They tsk tsk, they call you selfish. And then you wonder if they're right. And then you think that they *are* right: You are selfish. You don't deserve time for yourself, look at all you could be doing instead. That makes them feel better. Now they don't have to deal with the feelings that your taking time for yourself brings up in *them*. You are no longer a threat to their shaky self-concepts, to the parsimony in their lives. Good for you. Now you can binge again.

A woman who had taken a weekend workshop with me called me a few days ago. She said, 'I didn't realize how revolutionary this process is. I didn't realize how many people I would threaten by not dieting, by eating cake at lunchtime, by taking time for myself. I feel like I'm plugging into everyone's vulnerable areas and they're threatened and angry. I feel so alone.'

On a cultural level, dieting is easier than not dieting. Bingeing is easier than breaking free. Dieting and bingeing and complaining about your weight are accepted as the norm. Feeling good about yourself, eating what you want, and taking time to do what seems frivolous are not acceptable. There are too many people who unthinkingly accept the societally reinforced methods of losing weight but who also are aware, even if it's an awareness that is all but submerged, that they are in pain, that this system is not working. But it's scary to take a leap, to risk disapprobation and rejection, to become the target of people's frustration and pain. The question you must ask yourself is how long are you willing to endure your pain so that you avoid provoking theirs?

Before you can take time for yourself in ways other than bingeing, you must first ask yourself if you are worth that much. Do you deserve to have breaks in your day when you are doing nothing but what utterly pleases you and only you? Who would be affected by these breaks? How do you think they would be affected? Would they judge, reject, or dismiss you? Would they approve? Can they take care of themselves? What do you think of people who 'do nothing'? Did anyone in your family ever take time just for themselves, and if they did, what happened?

Deserving time for yourself is not a function of how smart or pretty or thin you are. Deserving time for yourself is not a function of how much you did or didn't accomplish that day. Deserving time for yourself is a function of the fact that you are alive and deserve to have time for yourself.

Make a list of things you love to do. Meaningless, frivolous, irresponsible things. And then, each day for the next week, do at least one of them for a minimum of fifteen minutes. *Then, make another list of your beliefs about bingeing and the actions that spring from such beliefs.* This list will provide the opportunity for you to 'name' the unspoken assumptions on which your actions are based. Once they are named, you can then ask yourself whether you want to keep acting from them or whether you want to replace them with more forgiving and healing beliefs.

Longstanding beliefs, however true they may appear,

are only based on information that was available to you when the belief was formed; with new information, you can change your beliefs. But it takes perseverance and, at the very least, a new belief that replacing beliefs is possible.

The physical component of bingeing, the way in which you eat and don't eat, also involves deprivation.

Not long ago I was watching three children play with a pencil. Each of them wanted the pencil. Each of them whined, cried, cajoled to get it. Soon another child arrived and two of the three ran outside to greet their friend. The third child was left with the pencil, after which he immediately lost interest and began playing with a toy. So much for the glamour of what you can't have and the ordinariness of what you do have.

If I walked into the room with a velvet-covered box and told you you could look at anything in the room except the box, what do you think you would do as soon as I walked out of the room?

We put food in a box, cover it with glitter and velvet, tell ourselves not to look, and then wonder why we feel such an urgent need to rip it open. We put food in a box, cover it with glitter and velvet, and then when we rip it open, we condemn ourselves for lacking willpower, determination, and discipline.

Sometimes we binge not because we want chocolate but because we're not allowed to have it.

When you let yourself eat *anything* you want whenever you are hungry, and I mean *really* let yourself – not trick yourself by saying, 'Well if you want ice cream, you can have half a scoop of Weight Watchers ice cream'; or, 'I know you think you want ice cream but ice cream is fattening so here's yogurt instead'; or, 'You can have vanilla but not chocolate because chocolate has more calories' – then the need to binge will slowly disappear. If you can eat whatever you want whenever you are hungry, then there is no need to eat it all now because tomorrow you're going to take it away again. Binges are last-ditch attempts to get *all* of what you want before you can't have it anymore.

A few words about food allergies. I have heard from many clients that when they are allergic to certain foods, eating them creates cravings for more of them and precipitates bingeing on them, while at the same time causing allergic reactions. If you suspect that you have food allergies, please . . . go to a nutritionist or health professional whose guidelines and beliefs you respect. Get a physical check-up so that you won't worry about hurting yourself.

Many people say that eating sugar precipitates a craving for it and subsequent bingeing on it. I have found this to be true and not true. What's true for me is that when I eat sugar on a regular basis, I want to continue eating sugar on a regular basis. I like sweet anything, and if I satisfy that craving for sweet with sugar, I'll usually want it the next day and the next. But I don't find myself bingeing on it – three bites is usually enough – because all I want is the taste of it in my mouth. What's also true is that I feel better when I don't eat sugar regularly. After two weeks of eating it daily, my body feels dull and I don't feel as energetic as I normally do. When I become aware of that dullness, I do a quick mental review of my recent food intake. If I notice that sugar has been part of my daily diet, I'll cut it out. The difference between cutting sugar out now and cutting it out when I was on a diet is that I am doing it out of choice instead of fear. I am not worried that if I let myself have two cookies I'll eat the whole box.

When you no longer put foods in a box and call them forbidden, you will no longer feel the urgency to rip the box open and consume what's in it in a frenzied race against the time when you'll slam it shut again.

But . . . when you've tried it all, you've done your best, and you still find yourself knee-deep in food, frantic and wanting to stop more than anything in the world but not wanting to stop more . . .

● **Sit down.** Wherever you are, sit down. If nothing else, you'll be able to taste the food better because sitting down will signal your brain that 'this is for real. We're actually eating now.'

● **Don't try to pretend that you're not eating.** Bingeing has a quality that makes it seem like an act caught in the middle, but not valid in itself. You might as well make it valid. You're doing it. Once you recognize, admit, and *accept* the fact that you are bingeing, you might decide to stop. You might also decide to continue. But until you notice that you are bingeing you have no chance of doing anything except what you're doing – cramming food down with a violence toward yourself. This may sound silly and elementary. You may be saying, 'Of course I realize when I'm bingeing,' but how many times have you dived into food and half an hour later emerged and wondered where you were when all this food was being consumed? That's what I'm talking about.

● **Give yourself permission to binge.** I get looks of sheer terror when I say this in a workshop because what immediately surfaces is the fear that 'If I give myself permission to binge, I'll never stop. Not ever.' Not true. The longer you deny yourself permission, tell yourself it's not okay, that something is really wrong with you, you will never get your life or body into shape, the longer the binge will last because your mind will be on the judgements, not on the food. The mechanics of lifting, chewing, and swallowing will go on without your attention while you are consumed in hating yourself. Once you give yourself permission, you can start tasting the food. And when you start tasting your food, you can relax. You can decide whether you *like* the taste of it, and, if not, whether you want to continue to do what you were already doing without your permission.

● **After you've given yourself permission and have focused your attention on the food, play a game with yourself.** Notice the texture, taste, and temperature of the foods. Notice how they feel in your mouth, going down your throat, in your stomach. You might discover that you don't like the taste of it or that it really doesn't feel good in your body. That it makes you too cold. Or too warm. Or you might discover that you do like the taste of it and want to keep eating it. Either way, you'll be in touch with your body and will be capable of deciding how much and what you want to eat so that you can *enjoy the binge*. As long as you are going to spend an hour bingeing, it makes sense to enjoy the food. Otherwise you're torturing yourself. If torturing yourself helped you stop, it might be useful, but it doesn't help you do anything but torture yourself more.

● **Get up from the table, floor, bed in the middle of a binge and go to the mirror.** Touch your face, your arms, your legs. Remind yourself that you're still there, present, alive. Though you've been totally focused on getting food into your mouth for the past half hour or so, you really are more than a mouth and more than your need to eat. Affirm that. Look into your eyes. Smile. If you want to return to the food, go ahead.

● **If you are alone, talk out loud. Talk directly to the food.** Tell the food you are bingeing on what you want it to do. Speak directly to it. You might tell it that it's supposed to be numbing you, knocking you out, putting you to sleep. You might tell it that you're eating it because you want to forget about an incident. Or that you need a treat.

Sometimes when you are in the middle of a binge, it's simply unrealistic to expect that you'll be able to get up and take a nap. Sometimes the fury of a binge, the momentum of it, carries you along and you don't care if you're eating because you want a nap and don't know how to give yourself permission to take one in the middle of the day . . . you're still going to eat.

When there's that degree of momentum already operating in a binge, I let myself act it out. There's a wildness to some binges that demands to spend itself through food and only through food. At that point there's nothing to do but let it, watch the feelings come up and stop when it's time to stop.

● **If someone walks in during a binge, don't try to hide your food.** You're not doing anything wrong. If they ask what you are doing, tell them you're eating. If you feel very comfortable with them, tell them you're bingeing. They might feel like joining you. Or they might look at you in astonishment and laugh. Or they might grimace. But no matter what they do, you're allowed to keep eating, if that's what you want. A friend of mine walked in last week and I was sitting at the kitchen table eating a bowl of ice cream; a half-eaten package of tea cookies was next to me. When he walked in, I said, 'Hi. I'm in the middle of a binge.'

After the binge . . .

● **It is crucial that you be KIND to yourself, that**

you be kinder to yourself now than you've been in a long time. This is when you need yourself most. Don't leave. You are most prone to self-condemnation, punishment, deprivation at this time, and if you let yourself fall into that trap, you'll be lost until you can muster the compassion to retrieve yourself.

Do something wonderful. Take a bath, go out and buy something special, take a walk, call a friend long distance, take a nap, buy a magazine. The something wonderful will counteract the deluge of self-condemnation. You need to let yourself know that you still believe in yourself.

● **Forgive yourself.** You did the best you could. If you binged and thereby did something that didn't immediately and obviously contribute to your happiness, it's because you didn't know what else to do. You're human. A teller at a local bank has a sign at her window proclaiming, 'Please be patient. God isn't finished with me yet.' She's probably not done with you either.

● **Take some time, either by writing or sitting or thinking, to** *learn from* **the binge:**

What precipitated it?

Was it a feeling you've had before? A recurring situation?

Imagine that same precipitating factor, but this time, in your fantasy, you are not going to eat. You are going to sit or stand wherever you were before you began eating and you are going to let yourself feel the feelings that were stirred up.

What are those feelings?

What is so frightening about letting yourself experience them?

What happens in your fantasy when you allow those feelings to surface instead of swallowing them with food? Now go on to do exactly what you did after the binge. How does the situation change (i.e., your feelings about yourself, others) when you don't binge?

If you had it to do differently, what would you change the next time around?

A binge is never wasted time if you learn from it. Learning from it takes you deeper into yourself, gives you clarity about your motivations, your needs, and helps you for the next time.

● **Do not deprive yourself of food the next day.** Your immediate reaction to a binge might be to restrict your caloric intake, possibly by fasting or only eating one meal or by going to three exercise classes. This is punishment. This is tightening the noose around a self that's already starving, refusing water to a self that is already dying of thirst.

Just as you need to be emotionally kinder to yourself after a binge, you also need to be physically kinder to yourself. You need to let yourself know that you haven't given up. When you get hungry again, ask yourself what you would most like to eat. And then give it to yourself. The best thing you can do after a binge is to eat again when you are hungry, but this time pay very close attention to the taste and texture of the food and to when you've had enough. You need a confidence boost. You need to be reminded that you can eat what you want and take care of yourself at the same time, that eating does not destroy you, that eating what you want will not make you fat. You need to know that always, but you need to know that now most of all.

Three months ago my father sent me a box of my favourite chocolates from Switzerland. Five years ago I would have either eaten it all in one night or eaten most of it in one night and thrown the rest away so that it wouldn't be there in the morning. Last week I had to throw the uneaten box away because the chocolate had lost its taste. Five years ago I would have given my right arm to be one of those people who can receive a box of chocolate, forget about it, and let it rot in the refrigerator.

Now I am one of those people. And I've still got two arms.

6
Family Eating: The Sins of the Parents

'They made me sit at the table until I finished the peas. When I wouldn't eat them, my brother put my face in them.'

A Breaking Free workshop participant

On Being the Parent

During the first few hours of a workshop, the participants introduce themselves and give a brief, weight-related family history. Fourteen out of every sixteen people with whom I work trace their difficulty to their childhoods and the messages they received about food and their bodies from their families. Many women watched their mothers dieting, saw and felt them sneaking food and feeling guilty about it while always trying to be thinner. Many heard from their mothers that they too should start being careful about what they ate, got scolded for eating cookies after dinner or sneaking candy to their rooms at night. Food was used as bribery ('eat your dinner and you can watch television') and as reward ('good for you, you've finished your vegetables, so now you can have dessert').

Because the dinner table is traditionally a gathering place at the end of the day, eating becomes associated with triumphs and tragedies and becomes so inextricably linked with them that its purpose — physical nourishment and emotional satisfaction — is overlooked.

Because how we eat is a metaphor for how we live, feelings about receiving pleasure, being nourished, taking time for oneself, and body image are also passed from parent to child. With intuitive wisdom, a child can sense how you feel about your body, and how you feel about your body will be a model for how she should feel about her body. That child will usually either emulate what she sees or rebel against it and do the opposite. In either case, the example a parent sets is a powerful determinant in patterns that will deeply affect their children for the rest of their lives.

When I arrived at the house of a new friend recently, her very heavy daughter was sitting in the living room. 'This is Geneen Roth, honey. This is the woman I told you about who wrote the book on compulsive eating. Tell her, Bobby honey, how well we've been doing on our diet this week.' She stopped for a moment, looked at me, looked at Bobby, and said, 'We've lost five pounds, haven't we, honey?' I wanted to put a rock, a candlestick, the cat, anything into her mouth before she said another word. Bobby sat there staring at me. She didn't move, smile, blink, or talk. After too much silence I finally said, 'I think it's terrific that you lost five pounds, Bobby, and I hope it means as much to you as it does to your mother.' When Bobby left the room, I grabbed my friend's arm and said, 'Don't you ever do that to me again. And I know she's your daughter, but if I were you I wouldn't do that to her again, either. That was horrible.'

She looked as if I'd slapped her. 'What was wrong with that? It's all true.'

So we talked about the fact that she had said 'we' when she meant Bobby, and that using the plural took the responsibility, power, and satisfaction away from Bobby's accomplishments. Then we talked about dieting, scales, and the need to respect what seemed obvious – Bobby's desire for privacy about what she eats. 'If your intention is to help your daughter,' I said, 'you're not. I give her five more years before she's sitting in a Breaking Free workshop telling the group about her insensitive, overbearing mother.'

It has often occurred to me when I listen to people talk about the melba toast their mothers packed for them at lunch or the way their fathers teased them about their hips that if parents knew the power they had to influence their children's attitudes about themselves, they would give more thought to the food rules, beliefs, and statements that fly so easily from their mouths and land just as easily in the guts of their children, where they stick and fester for a lifetime.

It's not my intention to blame parents for the food problems their children have or might have in the future. As parents, we do the best we can, however often we can do it. We do what we know how to do. A child takes what is said and makes it her or his own. How our words seep into the corners and crevices of another being, how they turn and develop and grow, depends on the person who is hearing them; two children can hear exactly the same thing and interpret it differently. What, of all we say, is heard and used, and why, of all we say, one thing sticks instead of another, is absolutely individual.

I do not want to, nor do I believe in, blame.

But I do believe in sensitivity and awareness.

My mother was a very fat child. And, as she remembers her adolescence, her fat was the source of her greatest shame. She tells a story about a hot summer day when she was working as a salesclerk and her legs, which were very big, were rubbing together and chafing, causing her so much pain that she couldn't stand up any longer. She called her mother and asked her to bring some lotion. When her mother arrived, she yelled at her in front of her co-workers and said, 'If you weren't so fat this wouldn't happen. Don't you think it's about time to lose some weight?'

When my mother was twenty-four she gave birth to my brother. On the day she was leaving the hospital, she and her father were waiting for the elevator to arrive and her father turned to her and said, 'Now, Ruthie, *now* are you going to lose some weight?'

She says today, 'I was so humiliated. I was married, had two children, and my parents were *still* telling me to lose weight. After that incident at the elevator, I went on diet pills and lost thirty-five pounds.'

It's not surprising that when she had a daughter who didn't turn out to be a long-legged, gangly tomboy, she was concerned, lest I repeat and re-experience the shame of her childhood. In her concern, she repeated her own mother's mistakes. She didn't yell at me in front of friends, but she let me know, both verbally and non-verbally, that because I was prone to being fat, I had to watch everything I put into my mouth. And watch I did. For her back to turn.

At eleven, instead of evaluating the situation myself, I externalized the responsibility for my weight, gave her the power to decide when I was too fat, what was thin enough, what I should and shouldn't eat. That in turn allowed me to sneak, binge, and eat continually when she wasn't around. My weight became an issue between *us* and not an issue that belonged to me, my body, my food.

My mother was afraid. She was afraid that if I ate what I wanted to eat I would be fat and I would be miserable. And I felt her fear; I fought with her about it, but I believed it as truth. We spent years battling about food, and I spent years after that battling with myself, talking to her, screaming at her, proving myself to her in my mind. Every time I lost weight I wanted to call her on the phone, and when I gained weight I didn't want to talk to her. If I felt fat and was supposed to go to New York, I didn't want to go. And often didn't.

Not long ago I spent a few days with her in New York. On the second day my mother said, 'I'm going to tell you something and I hope it doesn't make you upset, but you've gained weight. I can see it in your legs.' And I winced. It was true, I had gained about five pounds, but I felt fine abut it and knew that eventually, I would lose it. Hearing it from her changed the fact that I had gained five pounds. Suddenly I began worrying and doubting myself. I wanted to say, 'Do you still love me, Mom?' And then I wanted to eat. I wanted to open the cupboards and eat the cookies, the crackers, the jars of peanut butter, the five different kinds of dry cereal.

My mother had made an observation that I myself had already made. But when she said it, it was like throwing a hand grenade into my confidence about my looks and self-worth. Why, only days before, had I so airily dismissed the five pounds when I could see now that they were surely an indication that something was terribly wrong with my life?

When I saw that I was panicking, I went for a walk and got back in touch with my feelings about my body, how much I truly liked it, and that I thought it looked fine. Rounder, but still fine. On my walk I realized that I was still all the things I was before I'd gained the five pounds and that life was still as lovely and painful as it always had been. On my walk I realized that I wasn't fat. And I realized that my mother, at fifty-two, with a thin, shapely body, still thinks she's fat. Back at the house, I went to my mother who was sitting at the round linoleum table. I said 'Mom. I know you meant well, but please: Don't make any comments about my weight. It's too painful.' And I haven't heard a whisper on the subject again.

PARENTS . . .

● **Cannot protect their children from pain.**

● **Need to be very careful about what looks like protection.** It can often be a desire to protect themselves, not their children, from reliving their old but similar pain.

● **Can allow their children to take responsibility for food.** They can, from the time their children can talk and reason, consult them in grocery shopping and cooking.

● **Post a grocery list on the refrigerator.** Give each child their pick of two or three special items each week. This will instil in them the sense that their decisions and feelings about food are important enough to be considered and acted upon.

● **Allow them to decide on one or two dinners per week.** Enlist their help in preparing, cooking, and cleaning up. The more active a choice they have in shopping, cooking, and eating, and the more they see that their choices are valued, the more they will value themselves and trust their decisions.

● **Talk about nutrition, read books together, plan meals based on what you read.** Make the process interesting and flexible instead of rigid and authoritarian. Children want to learn; they are curious and they are interested. Use their interest to their best advantage . . . teach them the joys of taking care of themselves.

● **Do not use the dinner hour for airing grievances, arbitrating fights, disciplining, or emotional discussions of any kind.** When you sit down to eat, eat. Pick an agreed-upon time either after or before dinner to discuss what needs to be discussed.

● **If you set aside time together that isn't for eating, you will relieve the burden that's placed on the evening meal.** Sometimes, as children get older, schedules differ and are hard to coordinate with a set mealtime. I *like* family dinners but not as a substitute for closeness. Just because a family has dinner together every night does not insure intimacy. Too many dinner hours are spent in sullen silence or angry quarrelling. A family that does not eat together will not come flying apart if shared time is kept as a priority. Take a walk together, go to the park, a museum, a concert, a movie.

● **Establish a 'free night' once a week.** Everyone is allowed to eat *whatever* they want for dinner whenever they want it. Frozen pizza, coffee cake, popcorn – it's all permissible and no negative judgements are allowed.

● **'Bojangles'.** My friend Rick's family had a tradition they called 'Bojangles.' Once a year, the entire family, three children and the parents, would pile into their car and drive to the local ice cream parlour. There they would each pick a flavour, on a cone or in a dish, they wanted to eat. Ice cream in hand, they went back into the car, where they would sit and lick. After the first round of flavours was finished, they'd climb out of the car again and return to the store, where they would order a second round. Ice cream in hand, they'd pile back into their car, and when they were finished they'd pile back into the store. This would go on until no one could tolerate the thought of another lick.

When Rick told me this, I squealed with delight. He told me that they all looked forward to that night, talked about it for weeks before and for weeks afterward. As a family, it gave them something to look forward to, joyful time together, and permission to be outrageous.

Bojangles was a way of acknowledging *everyone's* – parents' *and* children's – need for exuberant frivolity. It's hard work to keep the child within us alive, but without that child's fresh vision, living can quickly become a series of 'shoulds' and 'have-to's.' Bojangles was not spontaneous, but it gave rise to the spontaneity of childish delight.

It also acknowledged our need to kick back on the nutritional level as well. It was a way for the parents to say, 'We know that carbohydrates and green leafy vegetables and proteins are good for you. We also know that it's a drag to eat them all the time. So tonight let's forget the rules. Tonight you can live out your fantasy. Tonight is for you.'

Smart parents.

The purpose of these exercises is to encourage your children to develop trust in their ability to care for themselves, respect for their health and their bodies, and a relationship with you in which they feel you are guiding and walking with them instead of judging them, preaching to them, and doubting their autonomy. But first you must pay close attention to your own fears about your body; if you don't believe that your body will tell you when and what to eat, it's going to be difficult to encourage that belief in your child. To foster a healthy relationship between your child and his or her body and food, you must also begin working with yourself on the issues of trust, body image, and self-worth. You don't have to feel resolved about them; you can still be in the process of learning. The basic requirement is that you remain open to discovery and that you don't present yourself as an authority. You have as much to learn from your children as they do from you.

I realize there's a delicate line between the desire not to pass your obsession with food on to your children and being concerned that if you let them choose what they want to eat they will subsist on a diet of Twinkies and hot dogs. But children are wise teachers when it comes to food. Friends and workshop participants with children notice that, before they get inundated with sugar so that all they want are lollipops and chocolate kisses, and before food becomes targeted with punishment and reward, children gravitate toward what their bodies want and need. One day they want only broccoli or apple sauce, the next day they want potatoes or cheese. They want it when they are hungry and when they have had enough they push it away because they haven't yet learned to substitute food for sadness or anger or fear. Watch them. Learn from them. And do your best to separate your fears about yourself and your body from their growing and vulnerable psyches.

I watch what happens to the members of a group who sense that one person, me, believes in them. The corresponding feeling of self-confidence that such belief brings is radiant. They begin taking care of themselves in ways they never believed were possible: eating what they want, wearing what they want, saying what they feel. They actually look different from week to week. Their eyes begin to twinkle, their faces look younger.

When they sense that I believe in them, they have permission to believe in themselves.

When your children sense that you believe in them, they can believe in and trust themselves. And they won't be sitting in my living room twenty years from now telling me how their mothers put them on diets when they were eleven.

One of the women in my eight-week workshop has three children. Since taking the Breaking Free workshop, she eats what she wants, she eats sitting down, she's begun taking time for herself. And her children are beginning to do the same. One of her children, a little girl, was eating sporadically and bringing home half-eaten lunches. Now, her mother allows her to choose from a variety of foods and as a result, her child comes home with no leftovers but her napkin.

A few nights ago they were sitting down to dinner and her daughter walked in with a poster size sandwich board strung around her neck: The sign in front said 'No more eating and reading' and the sign in back said 'No more eating what you don't want.' Her mother thought that was pretty terrific. So did I.

Returning Home

My mother remarked upon an interesting phenomenon a few years ago: My brother and I do the same thing every time we walk into her house. We walk straight to the refrigerator, open the door, and stand there, gazing. We open the freezer, the pantry, and then, when we're finished looking, we unpack our suitcases, sit in the den, and talk. No matter how long we've been away or how far we've been, the refrigerator is our first stop. 'And,' my mother said, 'it's not as if you were looking for something to eat. You just stand there and stare. The two of you are weird.'

When she brought it to my attention, I realized that something about the kind and the amount of food in my mother's refrigerator translates into security for me. In the house where I grew up stands the refrigerator I grew up around and grew round on.

Until four years ago, my trips to New York, whether they were two days or two weeks, were spent bingeing. During the week before I left, I'd worry about how much food I was going to eat once I got there, promising myself that this time would be different. One year a friend and I spent the entire night before I left making carrot-beet soup. We filled two thermoses with it and took them on board the plane with us. One of the thermoses promptly leaked onto my white dress, my friend's beige pants, and the powder blue skirt of the woman sitting next to us. The other one made it as far as my mother's kitchen sink, where, as I was spilling it down the drain, I was eating chunks of butter brickle from the local chocolate shop. I lugged not only two thermoses but a twenty-five pound juicer on the plane with me, determined to drink fresh carrot juice each day for breakfast and not stuff myself with Danish. The juicer was moved to the storage room of the basement within hours of my arrival, where it has been collecting dust ever since, and I spent the visit eating Danish and cheesecake from the delicatessen.

Returning to your parents' house can easily become a time of unconscious and bingey eating if you are not prepared to deal differently with the patterns that such homecoming triggers. If I am not aware of the pull, just walking into my mother's house signals: 'Walk to refrigerator. Open door. Eat.'

When I examined this automatic response, I discovered that:

● **For a week or so before my trip, I'd start worrying about how much I was going to eat once I got to my mother's house.** And sometimes, while I was worrying, I'd be eating to allay the worry. I'd worry about how fat I would get once I got to New York, and when I'd get to New York I'd already feel fat because of how much I ate in preparation for how much I was going to eat.

● **Eating – going out to lunch, dinner, family get-togethers – is the focus of much of the time we spend together as a family.** Because so much fuss is made about food, it's difficult to say to my aunt who has cooked a huge and very elaborate dinner, 'I'm sorry, Aunt Louise, but I've been eating big meals for lunch and dinner for the past three days. I realize you've been planning this meal for two weeks and cooking it for a week, but I'm not hungry.'

● **'This is my last chance to eat . . . '** hot pretzels from the vendor on the corner of Thirty-fourth and Seventh, hot pastrami sandwiches from Squire's delicatessen, butter crunch from the Chocolate Chef.

● **When I was feeling fat, I wouldn't want to make the trip.** I didn't want my family to see me so heavy; I was embarrassed and ashamed of myself. I didn't want old friends to see me and think I was ugly or feel sorry for me. On one or two of these occasions, I decided not to go. But most other times, I went, felt awkward, self-conscious, and ugly, and I dealt with those feelings in the same way I dealt with everything else – by eating.

● **Because the house was the scene for so much loneliness and so many eating binges in response to that loneliness, being there triggers the memory of those days.** It's like walking back into my high school and suddenly turning into the awkward, self-conscious girl of sixteen whose voice was too loud, smile was too toothy, and who, no matter how she tried, could never seem to say or do the correct thing. Those memories are like thick, suffocating fog that surrounds me when I am in the house. Sometimes I forget who I am now, so reminded am I of who I was.

The fact that I am miles away from my present life and current relationships reinforces the sense of suspended time. I am a daughter again in my mother's house. The fact that I am author, writer, group leader, friend takes second place to the primal relationship of mother-child.

Last year during one of my visits, I found myself becoming absorbed by my mother's pain in exactly the same ways I did when I was in high school. I spent two days eating exactly as I did when I was a child – frantically and incessantly – until I called Sara in Santa Cruz, who reminded me that I wasn't an eleven- or twelve- or sixteen-year-old and dependent on my mother.

Going home again evokes primal associations of food and eating, love and nourishment. It is no wonder that even the thought of it can set off a constellation of feelings and behaviour patterns that have little resemblance to how you live now.

You can remind yourself that you're no longer a child living in your parents' home if you:

1. Prepare yourself before you go. If it's difficult for you to remember who you are besides their child, bring along reminders.
2. Bring your favourite books, a favourite pillowcase. When you get there, begin a journal.
3. Get away from your parents at least once a day to do something you like doing. Take a walk, go

to a movie, meet a friend, take a bath. Spend time alone. Fill yourself up.
4. Call a friend back home. Make contact with your present reality.
5. Be choosy about what you eat. Eat when you're hungry, but eat what you want.

When I am in New York and have spent a few days eating too much, the feeling I get in my body – that it's filled with wet cement – triggers a set of old, familiar, and depressing reactions: I withdraw, complain about myself, look for approval wherever I can find it. I feel fat and ugly and miserable, I feel I've failed; I feel I'm back in high school again. As soon as I realize I'm feeling this – and that might take another day or two – I bring myself back to the present by paying close attention to what I eat and when. When I act on the power I have to make myself feel better, the feeling of being stuck in cement disappears.

The most essential thing in dealing with homecomings is to be aware of and respect the profundity of them. If you're not prepared (and by preparation I mean recognition that going home is not like going anywhere else; old feelings take you by surprise, overwhelm you, frighten you), these reactions usually find their way back to food.

Here are a few more suggestions to get you through homecomings with bright eyes and vitality instead of with a body that feels like it's been filled with concrete:

● **If you find yourself eating compulsively the week before your trip because you are worried about eating compulsively once you are with your family, begin making a list of your food intake.** Go back to the exercises in the first few chapters that facilitate eating with awareness (i.e., hummers and beckoners, rating yourself on a scale of 1 to 10) and do one or two of them every day. Bring yourself to the physical level of food and away from the fretting and worrying. Your concern precipitates your overeating, which precipitates your concern, which precipitates your overeating. Begin eating again in response to your body's needs and examine what it is you feel anxious about.

Talk to a friend about it. Or make another list: 'I am anxious about going home because . . . ' Spend half an hour with your eyes closed, fantasizing about your return. What happens when you walk in the door? What are your interactions like? What do you feel most vulnerable about?

As long as you're eating compulsively, your anxiety will be about food. When you stop, you leave room to discover the worries and concerns that prompt you to eat. When you discover what they are, they change. Because they are no longer secondary and unnamed fears, you can act on them instead of being ruled by them.

● **If there are numerous family occasions that centre around meals, take lots of walks between them.** Get outside, breathe, exercise. Remind yourself that your body can move as well as eat. Be picky about what, out of all the food before you, you eat. Although you may not categorize yourself as a finicky eater, you now have a chance to be like one of those gawky, gangly kids you grew up with whose mothers had to bribe them with milkshakes and cookies. Eat only what looks divinely delicious. There's no reason to have one of everything. You won't hurt anyone's feelings if you ooh and ah over one or two dishes instead of five or six.

If you are not hungry, you can either find a very thoughtful way to say so (e.g., 'This food looks delectable but I'm not at all hungry. Would you mind if I took a little of it home so that I don't have to miss it?') and not eat, or you can put a tiny bit on your plate and push it around, make it look like you're doing something. Or you can lie. I don't recommend lying as a long-term, effective resolution because I think it's important that you express your true needs and desires without shame, but many people have told me that they find lying helpful when they are afraid of hurting someone's feelings. A lie, in this instance, would be: 'My stomach feels a little queasy. I don't think it would be wise to eat.' Or, 'My doctor says that kind of food doesn't agree with me.' Or, 'I've been sick to my stomach and I'm just beginning to feel better so I'm not going to eat right now.'

● **If you take part in organizing family events, suggest that you do something besides eat.** Go to a park, a movie, a museum; show old family movies, bring out family albums, play Scrabble or charades. I realize this is a risky suggestion; when you're not putting food down your throat, it gives words a chance to emerge. And you may not be used to speaking about real feelings to your family. Playing games gives you a focus for your attention without making yourself miserable.

● **Hot pretzels on the corner of Thirty-fourth and Seventh are there every time I go to New York.** I feel that last-chance urgency to eat what's in New York only when I realize that I'll soon be back in Santa Cruz and I won't be able to eat hot pretzels. But when I am back in Santa Cruz, and not depriving myself of food that I like, wanting a hot pretzel on the corner of Thirty-fourth and Seventh never occurs to me.

It goes back to deprivation and the fear of not getting enough at a nameless time in the future when you are starving and needy and alone. If I'm not hungry for a pretzel when I pass the pretzel stand and get one anyway, I'm eating to store up for the time in my fantasy when I'll want it and won't have it. But in real life, when I'm back in Santa Cruz, there are so many good things to eat that it's often hard to choose what I want. There's so much of what I *can* have that I never consider wanting what I can't have.

When you find yourself caught in the fervour of having to eat it all before you leave because you won't have it anymore . . .

1. Remind yourself that there are good things to eat wherever you are.
2. Ask yourself if you are hungry.
3. Ask yourself if you are hungry for that particular item.
4. If the answer is yes, there's no conflict.
5. If the answer is no, you've got two choices: You can eat it anyway or you can decide not to. These are the moments that are most difficult. You know you're not hungry, but you can feel the urgency in your body that says, 'Go ahead. Quick. Before something or someone stops you. Eat it *now*.' The tension at these moments can be so unbearable that you eat to alleviate it. At this very moment, then, you need to find a way to tell yourself that this isn't your last chance to have good-tasting food. If you are absolutely stuck on having this particular item, bring a small cooler and take your favourite foods back with you. Eat them tomorrow or the next day, when you are hungry. Think of all the good food you eat at home. When you eat what you want, no matter where you are or what it is, and you give your attention to food, when you notice the taste and texture of it, when you let yourself be

satisfied, then there is no such thing as having to eat more and more because you won't be able to get it next week. Satisfaction is a total experience; when you are truly satisfied, nothing is missing. The idea of wanting it because you won't be able to have it next week is unrelated to satisfaction. Wanting is in the future; satisfaction is in the present. Wanting focuses on what you can't have; satisfaction notices what you do have and allows that to be enough.

● **I don't want my friends/family to see me this heavy . . . .** This one's a hard one.

A few years ago my mother gave a big party in New York for her fiftieth birthday and asked me to fly in for it. At that time, I was the heaviest I had ever been in my life. I knew that at this party I would see people I've known since I was very young, and who, when they saw me last, commented on how thin I looked. I was anorexic then and weighed ninety pounds. The thought of having to face these same people, having gained back more than half my body weight, was humiliating. I thought of telling my mother the truth or pretending I was sick or saying I had too much work to do. Finally I decided to go because it meant a lot to my mother and because, by that time, I had started to believe in not dieting and discovering the benefits of my weight. I wanted to stay in touch with that and feel good about myself despite my weight.

My cousin arrived having recently lost twenty-five pounds and wearing a size six. My mother, with her tiny hips and long legs, also wore a size six. I put on the tentiest dress I had and walked into the people-filled living room. Nobody came right out and said 'My God, you've gained sixty pounds since the last time we saw you.' But I watched their eyes, their expressions, and imagined the disgust that was behind them. I spent a miserable, self-conscious evening.

I don't have a bag of tricks to deal with situations like these. I encourage you to work with the pain and to take care of yourself through it. If you can stay with yourself when you are in pain, instead of leaving yourself by eating, you can use the pain as a vehicle of self-discovery.

The most difficult part of facing people is facing what you *imagine* they are thinking. Two things are true about people's judgements:

1. Most people really don't care what you look like. They might notice that you've gained weight and wonder why, but then they're on to the next thing. Most people are too worried about the way *they* look and what other people are thinking about them to spend much time on you. Or else weight isn't an issue for them and they don't speculate about why you've gained weight or notice how much cake you eat. To most people – those who aren't your intimates – you are merely part of the passing show.

2. When someone does think negatively about you, that judgement is a reflection of them and of their values; it has little to do with you.

   The only people who weigh you and find you wanting are those who are worried about their own weight. Only someone who has brown eyes and hates their colour would hate brown in someone else's eyes.

   I used to look at heavy people and wonder

how they could let themselves go like that. I used to find fat repulsive.

Now I look at overweight people and want to reach out to them.

When I stopped judging myself, I stopped judging them. My response to their weight is an indication of how I eventually learned to respond to my own – with tenderness and compassion.

Most of the pain of others' judgements stems from our belief that their judgements are true and from what we infer about ourselves as a result.

Leslie, a woman in a workshop, was telling the group that she didn't want to go home at Christmas because she was twenty pounds heavier than the last time her family had seen her. She said, 'They'll think I can't control myself. They'll think I'm an awful person.' I asked her what gaining twenty pounds meant to her. And she said slowly, 'That something is wrong with me.'

Leslie had taken her judgements about herself and externalized them into breathing reminders of her unworthiness. Facing her family meant facing the inadequacy she felt about herself. The worst part about seeing her family was not facing *their* feelings about her weight but *her* feelings about her weight. They don't have to live in her body. They can look at it, pass judgement on it, then move along. She is the one who has to wake up with herself, move through the day with herself, fall asleep with herself. And her opinions about herself will either make it easy to wake up or they will make it hard.

How much does your weight truly matter to someone else? And how long do you think they will hold it against you?

Will they wake up tomorrow thinking about how fat you are?

Will they eat their breakfasts and remember how fat you are?

Will they tell their friends?

And if they do, how will it affect their friends' lives?

In the past, when you've judged someone's weight, what exactly did you think?

How does that relate to your feelings about your own weight?

Did that opinion about them stay with you throughout the day? The week?

Did it affect your feelings about them?

How?

You're not a monster. And you haven't committed a sin of any sort. No matter how awkward or heavy or ugly you feel, you deserve to treat yourself with kindness and respect. Here are some reminders of how to be gentle:

● **When you are going to visit family or friends who haven't seen you since you gained weight, wear clothes you love.** If you don't have any that fit your present size, get some.

● **Before you get there, think about how you would act if you were thinner.** How would you walk? Talk? Eat?

Now walk, talk, and eat that way.

● **Before the gathering, do something nourishing for yourself, spend some time feeling good about yourself.** Remember that you are more than your weight. You are the person who listens and loves and talks and laughs and cries. And you also weigh a certain amount.

● **Once you are at a family gathering, find someone you like to talk to.** Find someone with whom you can have a meaningful conversation. Don't talk about how fat or miserable you are. Don't apologize for yourself. You don't need to apologize. You need to get past the superficiality of what you look like to the real stuff that happens between people: the contact, the meeting, the exchange of ideas as well as feelings.

● **If you're hungry, eat.** And eat what you want. No carrot sticks and celery when you want crackers and cheese. That will only make you feel like you have to hide — and it might precipitate a late night binge on all you wanted to eat but didn't.

7
Social Eating
at Restaurants, Parties,
and During Holidays

'It tastes better when it's off someone else's plate.'

A Breaking Free workshop participant

Of all the exercises in a Breaking Free workshop, the one that elicits the most vociferous response is our pot-luck. As soon as I mention that next week we're going to eat together, there is an uproar of dissension in the room. Everyone has something to say, something strong. Two weeks ago one woman said, 'I'm not paying good money to come here and pig out.' Someone else nodded her head. Another woman said, 'When exactly do we eat and how long will it last and what will we do afterwards? I don't want to come for dinner; I'll come when it's over.' Then, 'I didn't come here to eat compulsively. I came here to learn how *not to*.'

Mentioning eating together is like dropping a bomb in the room and standing back to watch where the pieces fly. We talk and talk and talk about eating and food and bodies, but as soon as the possibility arises of actually doing what we've been talking about, it is terrifying. Like taking your clothes off in front of a group. Nobody wants to, and they're furious at me for even suggesting it. For so many of us, eating is our private face. The entire area of food – how we eat, when we eat, the places, the urgency, the food itself – is the part of ourselves we keep for ourselves. Often it's the part about which we say, 'If they really knew how and what I ate they would be disgusted, they wouldn't love me . . . ' The nights of eating when everyone is asleep, the stolen bites, the secret trips to the refrigerator. The part of us that never sees day.

In a group that focuses on and reveals secrets, it is difficult to hide. It's easier to eat in front of people outside the group because then you can pretend. You can eat cottage cheese and salad and they will think you're on a diet. Then you can go home and *really* eat. Not in a Breaking Free workshop.

Many women are professional givers. When they are mothers, wives, and career women, eating becomes their spot of everyday relief, the only time they spend alone.

When I was younger I thought that being in love meant that I would have no secrets. Being in love meant giving up, giving away, surrendering. I wondered how people in love could stand to be parted for even an hour.

Then I began to fall in love. And for three weeks, I gave up, gave away, surrendered. Everything. On rare occasions it lasted three months. After which I'd start shrinking at the way he crunched on his morning cereal and the inconsiderate way he turned the pages of the newspaper. And I'd feel myself pushing away from him and thinking that his feet were too big and his eyes were too little, and he'd be bald in twenty years and I didn't want a bald kid so forget it. When the relationship ended, I'd blame myself, believing that I was cursed with being a Virgo and Virgos are too picky. No one ever told me, or if they did I had forgotten, that I was allowed to be in love and still be alone. Needing solitude was as much as saying 'I don't love you anymore,' and most of the time, that is exactly what I said when all I really needed was to spend some time alone.

A few years ago my mother said, 'There are some

things I never tell anyone, a part of me I keep separate from Dick, from you, from my friends. I need that.' I wondered then, just as I wonder now, if solitude were recognized and supported as our need for turning within and allowing ourselves to float in the warm darkness of ourselves, like a baby grows surrounded by darkness and fluid, I wondered whether there would be so many people eating compulsively in secret. I wondered if eating were a symbol for our need to have a face that no one sees.

After those who don't want to eat in the group express themselves, I tell them that I understand their reluctance. And that we're going to do it anyway. We choose the dishes that will be served and who will bring what. The afternoon of the dinner I invariably get three phone calls from participants who have suddenly and mysteriously been taken ill. I tell them to come anyway. And then the food begins arriving and the good smells waft through the house. The table is slowly piled with food of every colour and texture; the excitement in the room is almost palpable. We sit away from the table and do a quieting-down, getting-in-touch-with-your-body exercise. We talk about how hungry we are, how we feel about having so much food in the room, what the concerns and fears and anxieties are. And then it's time to eat. And we walk over to the table to look at and smell the food. Each person describes what they brought and its ingredients.

Then I tell everyone that they can pick three dishes they would like to eat, put them on their plates, and sit down. And the bottom drops out. 'Three? Only three? That's ridiculous. You're really taking this too far.' I ask what they expected of a compulsive eating group? That they would come and be given permission to pig out? And everyone giggles – yes, that's just what they expected. Because that's just what they do when they are around a lot of food and a lot of people: They go unconscious. Forget everything but getting the food into their mouths. As if they didn't have a choice. As if eating with others meant eating compulsively.

During dinner we do many of the exercises that are mentioned in previous chapters (i.e., putting your fork down between bites, concentrating on the taste, texture, temperature of food, checking in with yourself about your satisfaction level, leaving food on your plate) and some that I will mention in this chapter. The food is outstanding and the dinner turns out to be a highlight of the workshop.

The experience of eating with the group teaches people that they can eat in front of and with others and not be ashamed of consuming cake or cookies or potatoes or bread. It teaches them that they can experience the joy of sharing food as well as the joy of feeling good when it's over. If they can do it once, they can do it again. And if they can do it again, they can do it again. And again.

Here is a list of exercises, ideas, and suggestions to guide you in learning how to eat comfortably with others and like yourself afterward. They are designed to help you turn social eating – at parties, restaurants, buffets, and potlucks – into a joyful, self-affirming experience.

The Importance of Solitude

Recognize the place in yourself that belongs to no one but you, and allow yourself time for its exploration so that eating compulsively does not get tangled up with the need to be alone.

If we want to derive pleasure from social eating then we must also recognize the need not only for solitary eating but the act and the state of solitude itself. If we are to feel confident and balanced with others, we must first know confidence and balance within ourselves. And because the act of developing this confidence, which at the beginning can only happen when we're alone, is not valued in our culture, the need for it gets pushed underground and is expressed in distorted and convoluted behaviour. Stolen eating. Heart-pounding nights of eating whatever you can before someone finds you. Like the need for indulgence the need for solitude is not defined as necessary, and like indulgence, solitude therefore becomes linked with something that *is* necessary – food.

Although they are linked in this case, solitude and indulgence are not synonymous. Indulgence is a kind of 'wasting time,' the permission and the realization of the need to be unproductive. It's a way of releasing yourself from the routine demands of life. Solitude is not a forgetting; it is a remembering. It is the time you take to dive into yourself, to remind yourself that you are full and whole when you are not in relation to anyone else. You might spend the time pottering around the house, listening to music, lying on your bed, watering and pruning the plants, writing in a journal.

● **Eat at least one meal alone every few days** and pay careful attention to the entire process of eating, tasting, chewing, swallowing. Eat whatever you want, however you want it. Cold spaghetti, grilled cheese sandwiches. Notice what eating is like when there is no one to talk to, nothing else to focus on.

● **Eat alone in a restaurant.** Go to a place where you feel comfortable. Notice any self-consciousness you have about being alone. Do you think people are staring at you, wondering why you are alone? Do you think they are feeling sorry for you? (Notice the kind of prejudice *you* have about being alone: You may think others are feeling these things because *you* feel them.)

How does it feel to sit in a restaurant, a naturally social place, and be quiet? Take the opportunity to look around you. What do you see? Can you stay with yourself enough, without worrying what other people are saying, to notice what you think, feel, see?

How does the food taste? Concentrate on its texture and consistency, the spices in it. Can you taste it more when you are alone or do you enjoy having someone there to talk with about it? How does being alone affect your enjoyment of food?

Eat alone in a restaurant at least three times. The first two times, you may be too self-conscious to enjoy it. The third time, you'll know if you can enjoy the experience. If you can't, you can't. You still will have learned what it feels like to eat alone in a restaurant and you will have learned what you think of aloneness by being aware of what you imagine others are thinking.

● **Take some time every day to be alone** (fifteen minutes, an hour). Be silent and self-contained; if you want to think about an immediate goal – or a six-year goal or a lifetime goal – do that. Acknowledge yourself for the ways you are being and doing what you want. Acknowledge the part of yourself that is for you. Respect your need for privacy.

Restaurant Eating

I was out with some friends last week for dinner at a lovely French restaurant. When the bread came, I touched it and found it was cold. I turned to the waiter and asked if he could take it back to the kitchen and have it warmed. He said, 'Of course,' and one of my friends looked at me and said, 'I wanted warm bread but I would never have thought to ask. I guess that's what leading compulsive eating workshops gives you – guts.'

Eating out is a treat for which you are paying money. If you're not sure what's in a certain dish, ask. Establish eye contact with the person who is waiting on you; let them explain what they know. If you are pleasant but assertive, you'll find out what you want to know and it will help you make a decision about what you want.

When you are choosing a restaurant with friends, be clear about where you would go and what you would eat, given your first choice; your preferences and desires are no less important than those of someone who is five-six and 110 pounds. Say what you want and be prepared to compromise; sometimes you'll get your way and sometimes you won't.

If you get to the restaurant and you immediately don't like it – the ambience, the smell, the feelings you get when you're standing or have just been seated – don't be afraid to tell your companion. Everytime I've done this – opened my mouth (albeit with trepidation – it's embarrassing to say 'There's something strange about this place. I don't want to stay,' it seems ridiculous, inconvenient, hypersensitive) and said how I felt, my companion has agreed and we've left. And when I've been with someone who's said 'Let's go. I don't like it here,' I am always glad they've told me. Even if I don't share their perceptions, it's not pleasurable or relaxing to eat dinner with someone who is uncomfortable with the surroundings.

Once you decide to stay, look at the menu and choose what appeals to you *immediately*. Don't second guess yourself: 'Well, I really want a peanut butter sandwich but I can eat that at home, so I'll have salmon'; or, 'I'd like a hamburger but I've heard their speciality is sauteed scallops, so I'll have those.' You'll have salmon or scallops at the restaurant and when you go home or in the middle of the night you'll eat a peanut butter sandwich or a hamburger. Or you'll have salmon or scallops and won't feel satisfied so you'll keep eating and get fuller but not satisfied.

Other suggestions (some have been mentioned in previous chapters):

1. Don't talk about anything emotionally or professionally exhausting. Keep mealtime talk light so your body can work at dealing with food and not the psyche.
2. Allow some silence during the meal so that both or all of you can enjoy the food as well as the company.
3. Pay careful attention to your body's signal of enough. Remember that restaurant portions are not at all geared to the size of your stomach.
4. If you have food left over ask to have it taken away so that you don't pick. Or ask for a doggie bag.

Dinner Parties, etc.

If you're having people over for dinner and want to enjoy the dinner, don't eat it at the stove before they arrive. Ask someone else to take sips or leave the seasoning to chance. It's very tempting, very familiar, to stand at the stove and eat. But it's also possible not to do it if you are clear that you deserve to sit down and eat with gusto and pleasure in front of your guests.

If you're hungry, eat before you cook. Eat something you really want, something that will satisfy you.

Most of us get so involved in the preparation of party food, and are so full from nibbling by the time it's actually served, that we rarely enjoy our own parties. We're so concerned about everyone's liking the food that by the end of the evening we're exhausted from trying so hard. To compensate, we find our way back into the kitchen to eat what everyone else didn't.

When you find yourself either nibbling before a dinner party or attacking the leftovers later, you can of course ask yourself, What's happening? What are the assumptions I'm acting on about my right to eat a meal? (Is it that 'Meals are for thin people, not for me'?) Sometimes you can stop yourself for a few moments and bring the unspoken to the spoken level. And sometimes you can't. Sometimes the force of past habits may be so strong that it seems impossible to stop. You don't even want to stop; you don't care about becoming aware of why you're doing what you're doing. So don't stop; breaking free isn't meant to be physical or mental torture. But later, when you have quieted down, ask yourself if the food tasted good, if you enjoyed eating it that way. Ask yourself how your body felt while you were eating – was your heart pounding, did you feel as if you had to eat quickly? What about the meal itself – did you enjoy it? What kinds of feelings were you having about yourself and your body while the guests were there?

Be honest with yourself. Don't try to direct the answers one way or another. Maybe nibbling is truly enjoyable to you. Maybe you nibbled a lot at a time in your life that was particularly memorable or pleasant; maybe nibbling brings those memories back. The purpose of becoming aware of the decisions upon which you base your actions is not to change those decisions or those actions according to a preconceived idea but to discover for yourself if those decisions are still relevant and if the actions upon which they are based work well in your life.

When the meal is on the table, sit down with your guests. Look at the food you've prepared, really look at it. You planned it, you prepared it, now you can stop moving. If you are hungry, put what you want on your plate and eat it. If you're not hungry, decide how to best handle the situation. You could take a little or two or three items and try them. Or you could simply say, 'I'm just not hungry.' Whatever you do, do it so that *you won't feel deprived* and, when everyone leaves, find yourself in the kitchen, keeping the leftovers company.

When everyone leaves and there is food left over . . . you have a few choices. You can: (1) Clean it all up tomorrow. (2) Clean it up the night of the party. Carefully. If you are feeling deprived (i.e., you didn't enjoy yourself, you didn't eat what you wanted, you were too full when the meal was served so you didn't eat), this time is charged with binge tendencies. All that good food staring at you. And no one to watch how much you eat.

Here are a few suggestions to cut through what often feels like a magnetic force propelling you to the kitchen:

● After everyone has left, take some time for yourself. Do something soothing, something pleasurable. Take a walk, a bath. Sit in a rocking chair, read a magazine or a novel. Take your mind off food by realizing that you find pleasure in other things.

● If you are hungry (instead of wanting to be hungry), take a plate for yourself, put some food on it and sit down at the table and eat. Not standing and not off of someone else's plate.

● If you are not hungry but are determined to eat, take a very small amount of one or two items, put them on a *clean plate*, and sit down at the table to eat them.

● If you are not hungry but feel deprived and want to eat, remind yourself that you've got all this food in your kitchen to eat when you *are* hungry. And that will be sooner than you think.

If you are going to a party or someone's house for dinner . . .

● Wear something with pockets so that you have something to do with your hands besides reach for food.

● If you are famished before you leave, eat a small amount to take the edge off your hunger. (It's never a good idea to let yourself get so hungry you'd eat anything. You might arrive at your destination and discover that dinner won't be served for two hours.)

● If it's a buffet, go to the table and take some time to look at the food. What immediately appeals to you? If you are curious, ask what's in the food. People are usually appreciative that someone has noticed their work, and they are eager to talk about what they have spent time preparing. Begin by taking a portion of three dishes on your plate. You can go back for more if you want to, but start with three. This way, you can focus on the taste of those foods while giving yourself the message that you can contain your hunger instead of being overwhelmed by it.

Sit someplace in the room where you can eat instead of talk – you'll have plenty of time for conversation later. This is the time to taste and enjoy the food. You don't have to plant yourself alone in a corner and turn your back on everyone else, but you can be conscious of minimizing conversation and distractions in order to allow yourself the full pleasure of food.

If you're still hungry after you've finished the food that's on your plate, take some more. But limit yourself to three items again. You may not like the rigidity of this limit, but I urge you to try it. It provides a structure in a structureless and potentially overwhelming situation; it gives you something to fall back on when there's a table laden with food and you don't know where to begin and you want to eat it all. You can go back as often as you please and eventually try all that appeals to you. But begin slowly.

● If it's a sit-down dinner, and you don't care for some of the food being served . . . There are no set rules about social eating. There are some people who will get offended if you don't eat everything, others who take the refusal of food as personal rejection, as if by saying no to their food you were saying no to them. These people are not easy to deal with, especially if taking care of yourself (as well as or instead of them) is a priority. Sometimes taking care of yourself means saying no to someone like this and discovering that neither of you shatters. Sometimes it means compromising and taking a little bit, of which you taste an even smaller amount.

Whatever you do, remember that it is your body and that you have to live with the consequences of what you put into it. You have choices, and though the best action may be to eat some food you don't really want, you are making that choice for reasons you have considered and decided upon. If, afterward, you begin to feel resentful or angry, you can bring yourself back to the realization that you weren't *forced* into eating what you did but rather you *chose* to do so, and at the time, your reasons were sensible and appropriate.

● After dinner, whether it's at a buffet or sit-down gathering, choose someone you find interesting to talk to, thereby allowing the event to be about something besides food. Decide beforehand that you'll make contact with two or three people you don't know and then decide on creative ways to approach them.

Social eating has become the single way most of us spend time with our friends, family, and business associates. 'Let's have dinner'; 'How about lunch?'; 'Why not have a breakfast meeting?' It is over food that reconciliations take place, that long overdue contacts occur, that separations are decided upon, and important business decisions made, and in such cases, it is quite difficult, and almost absurd, to stay intent on lifting, chewing, swallowing, to consider the taste of food and how it feels in your body. But while the act of sharing food becomes a means to further a business or personal relationship, we shouldn't forget that while all this interaction is taking place, we are *also* feeding our bodies. And our bodies don't really know the difference between food mindlessly consumed and food eaten with awareness.

This is a gentle reminder: Food is for tasting and eating and nourishing. Food is not for when you don't know how to get together any other way. *Eating together* does not take the place of *being together.* If the primary purpose of a meeting is to talk, to spend time together, to decide upon mutual interests, there are other, more effective, and less fattening ways to meet.

When I first work with the participants in a workshop, they have a hard time figuring out when they are hungry or satisfied and what they really want to eat when they are alone. When they are with others, it usually becomes doubly confusing because of the added distractions of conversation and interaction. As I mentioned earlier, I feel it's important to learn to eat alone.

Not only because of the value of solitude but because it is quieter, and because it is easier to hear the subtle voice of your body when there aren't a lot of other voices speaking.

When you eat with others the focus changes from an internal experience – the moment-to-moment changes that tasting and swallowing and satisfying produce in your mouth and your body – to an experience that is both *internal* and *external*: the sensations in your body and being with another.

When I first started eating what I wanted and paying attention to food and my body, I found it almost impossible to eat with anyone else. I couldn't figure out how to taste the food or to know when I had enough and give my attention to the interaction at hand.

Many clients express the same difficulty. At the beginning it takes a good deal of concentration to focus on food when you're alone; being with others makes it that much harder. But not impossible.

There are a few things to keep in mind when you are eating with others. One of them is that, by definition, the experience will be different from that of eating alone, and it's unrealistic to expect that you will be able to pay such close attention to the eating process. What takes precedence in eating with others is the relationship, the sharing between you. And while that sharing is no more or less important than solitude and solitary eating, it is what you are doing at that moment and it has many joys of its own.

When you are eating with others, I suggest that you put your silverware down from time to time during the meal to give your full attention to what else is taking place. I also suggest that at some point, you excuse yourself and go to the restroom to give yourself time away from the food and interaction, time to ask yourself how you are feeling, if you want more to eat. In your own way, you need to find the subtle balance between eating with others and not losing yourself.

Breaking bread with friends and family can, on the deepest level, symbolize sharing the wonder of being alive. We really do need food to live. Food nourishes our cells, gives us energy, allows us vitality and radiance. A few weeks ago I was sick with a bad case of flu. I had a fever, a cough, and a sore throat. For what must have been the first time in my life I lost my appetite. As the days passed and I still couldn't eat, I felt myself getting weaker and weaker, getting listless, and not caring about things and people I usually care passionately about. I realized (again) how being hungry is a sign of life and how when we lose our appetite for food, our appetite for living follows close behind. It made me very sad to remember the times I've cursed my hunger, wished it would go away, wished I could be one of those people who push food aside, who lose their appetite when things get rough. Because there I was, one of those people, and it felt like death because I couldn't move and I didn't care. I wanted my hunger back.

When we eat we are taking part in an act that affirms life. And when we share the same food, we are ritualizing that act. We are hungry, we are alive, we are together.

8
About Exercise
and Scales

'Dear Bubbles,
   I'm glad you will be my friend. I weigh eighty-eight pounds. Maybe if I don't eat dinner for the next week, I could lose five pounds. If I weighed eighty-three, I'd be so much prettier.
   See ya later.'

My first entry in my first journal when I was eleven

The-Five-Days-a-Week-or-Else Syndrome

When I was about eleven or twelve, I stopped thinking that playing outside – tag, jump rope, hopscotch, hide 'n' seek – was fun. I started playing with Barbie and Ken, fantasized about kissing Robbie Levy, and wondered what Robert Alsworth looked like in his pyjamas. I became what my mother now refers to as a lump. Throughout high school, I hated gym. I thought the gym shorts were ugly, and I found every excuse to get out of moving my body.

When I was twenty-five, my friend Alice introduced me to a dancer in New Orleans, Leif Andersen, who taught classes in the style of Isadora Duncan: free-flowing and expressive movement that allowed the music to dictate the steps, Leif's classes put me in touch with the grace and the power of moving my body. Since then I have been enrolled in dance classes that have run the gamut from tap to African dance to aerobics.

I love moving my body.

Except when I don't.

In a recent workshop, one of the members said, 'Before I got this urinary infection, I was taking an aerobics class five times a week. Then my doctor told me I couldn't exercise until it had cleared up. It's been three weeks and I haven't gained a pound. I don't ever have to exercise again.'

And I said, 'That's right. You don't ever *have to*. If your only reason for exercising is not to gain weight, there are less strenuous ways to accomplish that goal.'

But I remembered the night, months before, when she had phoned me, upset by the sluggishness she felt in her body; she couldn't think of a thing that would make her feel as good as eating. I suggested getting out of the house and moving her body by walking or bicycling or dancing. And she signed up for an aerobics class that met three times a week. The next time I spoke with her she was thrilled by the difference in her body; she felt light and she felt strong.

Something had gone sour, very sour, between then and the night she spoke at the group.

The same thing happens continually with women and their bodies. It's part of the eternal quest to be thin. No matter what we do – if it relates to our bodies – it always gets translated into, 'Well, yes, it feels good, but think how much better it would feel if I pushed a little more and lost two inches off my thighs.'

If some is good, more is better because if some is good, maybe more will bring less flesh.

Exercise is a lure the way dieting is a lure: They both hold the promise of thinness if only you stick rigidly to 'the programme.' In a short time the freedom (from misery and size 16s) that exercise promises turns into the dailiness of prison bars. No longer a matter of desire, exercise becomes a matter of necessity, an act upon which your well-being depends.

We fool ourselves if, when we give up dieting and turn instead to exercising, we think we have broken free. We have in fact exchanged one kind of rigidity for another.

When you turn exercise into a 'have-to' rather than a 'want-to,' you take the strong and healthy part out, you take the joy out, you make it an endurance test, just another act in the long line of other grudgingly performed acts that you have to do because you have to be thin and you have to exercise to be thin.

Exercise has many physical and psychological benefits: cardiovascular fitness, increased endurance, feelings of strength and power. On days when I'm depressed and lethargic, a dance class picks me up, gets the blood moving, makes me feel alive again. But inevitably the day arrives when I am tired or on the verge of getting sick, when I have too much to do or an appointment that can't be made at any time except during the hour of my regular dance class, and along comes the thought: I've *got* to dance today, I ate too much last night, I've got to burn off 500 calories.

That compulsion. Not listening to my body, or to how I'm feeling, but driving myself, moving with an urgency that has little to do with the reality of the present moment. Compulsion is being afraid that everything – my looks, my well-being, my relationships – hinges on going to five classes a week.

When I stopped dieting, I didn't know how I would live without having the structure of a diet. I was afraid my life would shatter if I didn't hold it together with a diet; I felt lost.

Sometimes, when I realize I won't be able to dance that day, I feel lost again. I wonder what I will do instead, how much weight I will gain.

The danger of compulsive exercising is that we begin to rely on something other than ourselves to monitor our 'goodness' and our 'badness'. We're good when we exercise and bad when we don't. If we want to lose weight, we have to work harder. If we don't lose weight, and we've been depending on the workout to do it for us, we rebel and won't go for a week or two.

The danger is that it takes our choice away. And our hard-earned power. Whenever I realize that I've become identified with and dependent upon my class, I force myself to remember that my life will go on and I won't fall apart or gain 100 pounds if I stop going for a few days, a week, or even a month, that I am more than the shape of my body and that even if I did gain weight, I would be fine.

Breaking free is the moment when, after wrestling with my despair, I can say, it may be true that I am giving up the chance today to burn off 500 calories, calories that might add some weight to my body, weight that might add unattractiveness to my body, unattractiveness that might add misery to my life, but today, taking care of myself means not exercising, so I'm not exercising.

These are the warning signals that indicate compulsive exercising:

● You get so used to your exercise routine that even very important events are intrusions. You start fitting your life into your classes instead of fitting your classes into your life.

● What you eat or don't eat depends on whether you are exercising or not.

● You don't feel 'right' or 'complete' or 'good' unless you exercise.

● You exercise even when you feel sick or tired.

● It's beginning to be hard to drag yourself to class. You think of ways to get out of it; you hope you'll get pneumonia; you don't like the people who stand next to you in class; you want to punch the teacher in the mouth.

What to do about the warnings:

● Listen to them. They are a sign that something has gone wrong.

● Don't go to your class for a day or a few days. Take a walk instead or sit in a rocking chair for an hour and do nothing or read *Big Beautiful Woman*.

● The next morning after you skip a class, notice that although you didn't burn off 500 calories the day before, you have not suddenly gained ten pounds. Keep noticing.

● Remind yourself of all the things you are besides your body. Make a list. Begin it with 'I am . . . ' and don't allow any negative judgements about your body to creep in or on. In case you forget, you are worthwhile, you are caring, you are growing. To name just a few attributes.

● Eat when you are hungry, eat what you want, stop when you're satisfied. Remember that your body *does not want to destroy you* and will not go haywire as soon as you let down your guard. Trust that the two of you are working for the same end – your health, your happiness, your peace.

The I-Refuse-to-Be-a-Jane-Fonda-Clone-So-I'm-Not-Even-Moving-My-Left-Finger Syndrome

When Sara and I park two blocks from our destination, it's one and seven-eighths blocks too far for her. Sara doesn't understand what the big deal is about exercising. Her mother, she says, never exercised and has lived a fine healthy life. She says people have become neurotic about exercise. She says she thinks a lot of women exercise so that they can eat more and that 'that makes two compulsions – exercise and food – instead of one.'

I sit with my elbows on the kitchen table, dressed in my leotard and tights while Sara raves on about exercise. I understand why she feels what she feels. After all, I spent the years from eleven to twenty-five thinking that anyone who ran when she could walk was a maniac. 'But,' I tell Sara, 'exercise feels good. It puts little bothersome things in perspective. It's a place I can let loose, spend all my physical and mental energy so that I feel clean when I leave.'

When I go to a 5:30 class after writing all day and before leading a workshop in the evening, the workout is so strenuous that my thoughts fade into the background. I get into a purely physical, almost animal-like state: sweating, breathing, sweating, breathing, a state in which words don't count. When I leave the class, I feel as if I've been given another day because my energy is new. I *like* the feeling of working my body – that's not pretend and it has nothing to do with being thin. I liked it as a child, too, playing jump rope and volleyball and tag. But as an adolescent, I thought being athletic was unfeminine and jockish. Girls watched, girls cheered on the sidelines in teeny skirts while boys ran and sweated and developed confidence in their physical power and learned the joy of exertion, of trying to go beyond physical limits.

When, at twenty-five, I started moving my body, it was in a class that encouraged me to respect its impulses and desires to move and dance and fly. Slowly, I learned to appreciate the feeling of my body's getting stronger, of watching muscles define themselves. A growing sense of power accompanied these changes as I felt myself more connected to my arms and legs: We could move as a unit now; I was becoming my body's friend.

If, instead of being supported and encouraged to move for the joy of it, I had gone to an aerobics class in which the teacher talked about lumpy legs and cottage cheese thighs as we did the hundredth repetition of an abdominal exercise, I probably would have felt discouraged and critical of my body and would not have gone back for more.

Appreciation of movement is learned through direct experience. Being told 'it's good for you' isn't good enough. If you're causing yourself mental and physical anguish because you're trying so hard, let it go for a while. Or spend time sampling different kinds of movement and physical experiences. They are as varied as foods and it is possible to find the ones that hum to you.

I applaud the recent swing toward women's sports, but I feel that the link between fitness and thinness must be cut. If you exercise to get thin, the implication is that the way you are now is not good enough. This engenders a slew of critical judgements that eventually lead to frustration, hopelessness, and a decision to forget the whole thing. Negative judgements almost never lead to long-lasting change. If you are exercising because it makes you feel radiantly healthy *now*, then you are not involved in any sort of catch-22. You are moving because you like yourself. It is the difference between punishing yourelf and taking care of who you already are.

Some Suggestions
for the Saras of the World

● You don't have to feel like a pariah because you don't like exercise when so many others are embracing it. But be beware that what you might be taking pride in is the gratification of being an anti-exercise activist in our jogging universe.

● The only way you are going to discover the benefits of exercise is if you try it for more than fifteen minutes every six months.

● Begin slowly and with a form of movement that appeals to you.

● Exercise should be fun *while* you are doing it – not just after it's over.

● Be wary of classes that emphasize being thin. Avoid being critical of yourself or putting yourself in a harsh shape-up environment.

● If, after all of the above you still don't like moving your body, don't keep forcing yourself.

Scales Belong on Fish

I tell a 'scale story' to my workshops that speaks for itself:

My friend Sue is thin. She doesn't think twice about eating sandwiches with two pieces of bread, downing orders of french fried onion rings, and drinking Coca-Cola by the gallon. Sue works in a doctor's office, where she occasionally weighs herself. One day she weighed five pounds less than she had the previous time she'd checked. Sue was quite pleased with herself and on her lunch break, she admired herself in the window of every store she passed, bought herself a new outfit, and treated herself to a highly caloric lunch. The next day at work, the doctor told Sue that the scale was eight pounds off . . . in the wrong direction. Not only had she not lost five pounds, she'd gained three. When she called me, her clothes were suddenly feeling tight and she was conscious of a roll of fat over her belt. 'I need to go on a diet,' she wailed, 'I can't believe how fat I am.'

This was a thin person talking, someone who is basically confident about her body.

If scales have this effect on her, if scales can radically change her feelings about her body from one day to the next, consider the mental and emotional fluctuations scales can create in someone who is less confident.

Scales have the power to turn a previously depressing day into one with sunshine, and a previously bright day into a miserable one. When we get on a scale, we say, 'Tell me, machine, how I should feel about myself today.'

We've made the scale our symbol of authority, of worth, of truth. If we've been 'bad' there's no denying it because it shows up on the scale. If we've been 'good' getting on the scale will be its own reward. The scale, like God, knows all.

A scale, however, is just a scale – a cold, lifeless piece of metal – until we *give* it its power. We make it into the instrument that tells us if we should like ourselves that day or not. And we do that by accepting societal beliefs about the goodness and the rightness of being at a lower rather than a higher weight and also by continuing to weigh ourselves day after day. As if you can't tell by the way your clothes fit whether you've lost or gained weight. As if you need punishment to force you into losing weight. As if you weren't a feeling, thinking, capable human being who can decide for yourself what kind of day you're going to have and how you're going to feel about yourself.

Throw your scale out.

Or paste your ideal weight on it so that when you ask if you're allowed to feel good about yourself that day, it says 'of course.'

9

On Wanting:
If You Don't Let
Yourself Have It,
You Can't Lose It

'When I'm fat, people don't respect me. But if
I get thin, they'll be afraid of me because then
I'll be perfect.'

A Breaking Free workshop participant

'Because although Eating Honey *was* a very
special thing to do, there was a moment just
before you began to eat it which was better
than when you were, but he didn't know what
it was called.'

From The House at Pooh Corner

This chapter is about yearning for all that we don't
have. All that we don't have and think that if we did
have would bring us happiness and completion and love.

A house, a car, a promotion. A person – in a relationship that is loving and mutually supportive.

A body that is attractive. A body that is thin.

There is a fragile balance between the necessity to
have dreams and to move toward them and the distor-
tion of those dreams, between having dreams and living
in a fantasy of life . . . life that is always a step removed
from present reality.

When we want, we can dream about what it will be
like when we have. When we want, we create the beginnings, the middles, the endings of our dreams. We're in
control.

If life, of course, the dreams of other people, along

with their fears and their angers, are half of any outcome.

When we spend our lives wanting, we can dream
about how it will be when we get exactly what we want.
That incurs no disappointment. No risk, no vulnerability, no chance of being hurt.

When we spend our lives in the present moment, with
what we already have (the other side of wanting), we
lose control. The things we love get lost or shattered or
stolen. People leave us. People die. As soon as we realize
the preciousness of what we have, we realize that someday we might lose it.

Wanting to be thin.

There is a huge difference between being at a lighter
weight and wanting to be at a lighter weight. In fantasy,
being thin changes your entire life. Being thin allows
you to feel good, to feel pretty. Being thin changes your
dress size and with it, your wardrobe. Being thin brings
people close, attracts the long-awaited relationship.
Being thin gives you credibility. In a fantasy about
being thin, you stop wanting and become the wanted.
And then, something happens that you didn't plan on –
you lose control.

What happens when our bodies change and our perceptions don't?

When I weighed 120 pounds, I dreamed about weigh-
ing ninety, and in my dream, I was fluid and languid
and sensual. I was self-assured; I dressed in stylish
clothes. In my fantasy, being thin enabled me to concentrate on other areas of my life, areas that, at 120 pounds,
I was ignoring because of my intense preoccupation
with weight.

Then I lost thirty pounds and instead of becoming
fluid and languid and sensual, I shrank from physical

contact. I wore baggy clothes that hid my arms, my breasts. My thin self was only a dream; I never expected her to come to life, and I hadn't prepared her for daily events, only peak experiences. She knew how to glide into rooms, how to smile, sparkle, and attract attention, but she didn't know how to talk, work, feel.

When I lost thirty pounds, I felt as if my skin had been ripped away, exposing my nerves and muscles and bones. I was raw, vulnerable, constantly afraid.

A year and a half later, the awkwardness and ugliness I felt at gaining back fifty-five pounds were a small price to pay for the relief of knowing how to be. My weight gave me a role again; it provided me with a personality that was as familiar as an old shoe and on which I could blame every failure of my life, while I dreamed of the success I would have when I was thin again.

For you, of course, being thin will be different. You will be able to handle it, you will know you are thin when you are thin and you will be happy. You will wear clothes that tastefully emphasize your slimness. The intense preoccupation with your body will be gone and you will be able to concentrate on other areas of your life. And you will be fluid and languid and sensual.

Which is exactly what wanting is about: the persistence in believing that getting what you want will change your life, no matter what the evidence. This is never more apparent than in people who lose significant amounts of weight two, three, and four times in their lives. Though they find being thinner either difficult or not what they expected, and gain back the lost weight, they persist in reestablishing it as the goal that when achieved, will make everything better. They say that due to specific circumstances (which have since changed) they could not keep the weight off, but next time, next time will be different.

It's the wanting we want. Not the having.

During the first night of a workshop, when we go around the room and the members give a brief history of their weight and feelings about food, the passion of the desire to be thin is unbelievable. People describe wanting to be thin as 'consuming their lives,' 'intense,' 'overwhelming,' 'the thing beside which everything pales.' Words that are usually used to describe a love affair or reason for being alive.

Wanting to be thin pushes reality to the outer edges, dismisses it as only temporary until the real you, the essential you, can show your face. Whereas wanting to be thin is consuming and passionate and selective, being thin is like having corn flakes for breakfast and going to work. It's pleasant when you're slipping into a new party dress, but there are still bills to pay, dishes to be done, and a life to be reckoned with. You must still learn how to give love and how to compromise, how to say no and how to risk failure. You still have to make sense of the conflicts within you and, inevitably, someone you love disappointing you. During all those years of wanting to be thin, you put your life on hold and created a cushion between you and the aspects of living that were not in your control. Wanting to be thin protects you from the unfairness of life; it funnels the grief and sadness and pain of being alive into the grief and sadness and pain of being overweight.

When you spend your life wanting, you never get down to the actuality of living.

It takes great courage to admit the possibility that while you would 'die to be thinner,' you might not *want* to be thinner. Wanting loses its seductive power when you recognize that it might trap you instead of free you. When you can see being thinner for what it will be – not just a smaller body but a life lived in the muck and glory of the present rather than in dreams of a gilded future – the wanting will be stilled.

A woman in a workshop asks, 'Where does questing end and wanting begin?' How do our aspirations to express in the fullest and most satisfying way the best of who we are, differ from wanting?

A quest, it seems to me, stems from an intuitive belief that the key to our wholeness lies in the expression of what we've glimpsed in ourselves but not yet touched. A quest is connected to the you that reaches beyond itself to the thread that connects one human being to another. Questing is an expression of courage and vulnerability; wanting is an act of isolation and fear.

For many of us, wanting to be thin, like questing, comes from a desire to be our best selves, to have the energy locked in obsession available to us for work and relationships. But the act of wanting is in itself so powerful and complete that it isolates rather than stretches us.

When I ask the participants in a group to estimate how much time they spend wanting, the answers range from about 50 percent to 95 percent of their lives. Which means that by the time they die they will have spent *at least half* their lives in shadows, wanting without having – and dying without living.

Yesterday I took a walk on the beach at sunset. I was walking on the hard part of the sand, the part near the water, remembering what I'd once heard Joseph Goldstein (author of *The Experience of Insight*) say: 'We're intensity junkies. We think we have to be wanting. We think we have to be overwhelmed with feeling and desire and passion to feel alive, when this' – and he pointed to his body – 'is an incredibly complex and fascinating energy system. As it is. Without anything added.' As I walked, the lights of the boardwalk began to twinkle, washing the shore in a blaze of metallic gold. 'Appreciating what we have,' Goldstein said, 'is like going from the zap of drinking Coca-Cola every day to the subtlety and softness of drinking green tea.'

What To Do About Wanting Besides Having

On a practical level, it is important to put wanting into perspective by examining how it actually feels to want. The fantasies it creates and how those fantasies keep you trapped in endless cycles of more wanting. You need to examine honestly and carefully the components of wanting and how you perpetuate it.

● **List-making.** If you are not in a workshop specifically directed at compulsive eating, I would suggest that you make these lists either with friends or in some type of support group. Ask one person to say the title of the list out loud and as answers come, say them aloud as well. If someone's answer is also true for you, write it on your list. When you hear answers that don't fit you, don't write them down. Don't think about or censor anything. This isn't a test; you are doing this for yourself.

Take about fifteen minutes to complete the following five lists:

1. *Things I Want That I Don't Have* (a new car? a thin body? a different job? a new relationship? a baby?)

2. *Things I've Wanted That I've Gotten*
3. *Wanting Allows Me To . . ?* What does wanting give you? How does it help you? Does it give you a goal to always be working on? Does it give you a pleasant fantasy? Does it protect you from disappointments by keeping you locked into a fantasy?
4. *How My Life Would Change If I Got Those Things* (Do this quietly and by yourself.) Go down your list and next to each item you want, write a brief description of what would happen if you got it. Be specific. And honest. If you feel that having a baby would give you the chance to really love for the first time in your life, and in so doing would complete you, write that. Don't hold back, no matter how dreamy or romantic or ridiculous your imaginings sound. Better to get them on paper and look at them instead of holding them inside as vague, dreamy impressions.
5. *How My Life Has Changed Now That I Have What I Wanted* (Do this as quietly as you did 4.) Especially note things that have brought long-lasting happiness.

After you've made the lists, look them over carefully. Check reality against fantasy. Think about people you know who have gotten the things you want. Are they happy? Do they have what you think having would bring you? And what about the things you already have? Did they do what you had hoped? For how long? What happened to the wanting when it changed to having? Do you think next time will be different? How?

Talk about these thoughts and discoveries with your list-making friends. Are their experiences similar to yours? What can you discover about wanting from your own experience?

● **Assume a wanting position with your body.** Sit down in a chair and think about something you really want, something you are sure will make you happy. With your arms in front of you and both hands extended, reach for it. Reach. Keep reaching.

Hold that position.

How long can you stay that way? Why? How do your arms feel, your back? How is your balance? How strong do you feel when you are reaching?

Is it ever comfortable, even at the beginning?

This is the posture you are assuming emotionally when you want with intensity.

It hurts.

● **Tomorrow, when you wake up, imagine that your body is absolutely fine the way it is.** What happens? Remind yourself throughout the day that you already have what you want. Now what? Where does your attention go? What takes the place of wanting? What is the morning like when you aren't always wanting something you can't have? The afternoon? The evening? What is the crescendo of the day when wanting is absent?

10
On Having

'I've only ever been at my "perfect weight" once in the last fifteen years and only ate one tiny tiny meal to do that and I was as miserable then as I am now. More.'

A Breaking Free workshop participant

'I would die to be as thin as I was five years ago when I would have died to have been thinner.'

A Breaking Free workshop participant

At every public reading of *Feeding the Hungry Heart*, I've been asked to read the section about Michael, an erstwhile friend who, over a bowl of fettucine, told me that he found me unattractive because I was too fat. When I tell him that I think it's his problem, not mine, and who is he to talk, pudgy as he is, everyone laughs and applauds. They're glad I tell Michael, in kind but no uncertain terms, to get lost. They know what it's like to be told that they're too fat.

But there is an addendum to the Michael story: Six months later, when I saw him again for the first time after the fettucine incident, I had lost fifteen pounds. And he didn't notice. Michael, who had said that I was too fat, *didn't notice* that I was very thin. Knowing that I was as thin as I could comfortably be and sensing that his reaction to me was the same as it had always been was both relieving and painful. Relieving because it verified what I believed but could never prove about attraction: that it was to my style of walking, talking, laughing, expressing, thinking, and listening that someone was either attracted to or not. Liking the way someone lives his or her life is what seems to me to form the basis of attraction – that and how his or her living affects your living. When I saw Michael again, I realized that there was nothing I could do to draw him closer; he simply was not attracted to who I was and how I lived. And relieving as it was to have an intuitive belief verified by experience, it was also very painful. Because if it wasn't just my body, it was something less controllable about me that he found unattractive. Something in the fibre of my being, as much a part of me as the colour of my eyes and the texture of my hair.

When I went home that night, I looked in the mirror for a long time, trying to figure out what Michael found so unattractive. I studied my skin and my eyes, my hair and my mouth. I walked toward the mirror and away from it. I smiled, I stared, I laughed. *Why* didn't he find me attractive? The pain was sharp and I fell asleep crying. I didn't want Michael; I wanted to be attractive.

Since then, when by all reasonable standards I have been considered thin enough not to be overweight, that situation has repeated itself a few times with different people – potential friends as well as lovers. Each time, the pain is sharp. Each time, a voice in me cries, 'Why don't you want me?' which soon turns to 'What's wrong with me?' And each time the pain leads to a frantic attempt to convince someone to love me – a challenge fraught with urgency and anxiety. If I lose, I am not worth loving; if I win, my self-image is secure. The stakes are very high in this game: I'm fighting for permission to feel good about myself.

When I weighed 145 pounds, it was different: I was prepared. If I was rejected, I knew why. When I weighed 145 pounds, it was my fat that was rejected – not me. My fat was what surrounded me, protected me, hid me, but it was not me. I was inside. I was soft and vulnerable and sexy. And I was thin. I was a wonderful delicious secret. If at a party no one approached me, it was because they didn't know, couldn't see the secret of me beneath all that flesh. Not because they saw the secret and still turned away. Not like Michael.

One afternoon during the time I was heavier than I am now, I was lying on the bed with two women friends. As we talked, it occurred to me that they were brave to be thin. It was as if, in being thin, they were revealing the bones of themselves. They were wearing their insides on the outside, where everyone could see and either accept or reject them. I wondered if they knew how courageous they were. I wondered if I would ever be that courageous again.

When I weighed 145 pounds, I was in control. People couldn't reject me; I had already rejected myself. I knew I was too fat. I knew I was unattractive. They couldn't like me any less than I already liked myself. Each time I felt rejected, my secret self, the vision of who I was under all that fat, caught me. Like a net underneath a tightrope, it kept me from smashing to the ground. If they saw *me*, it would be different, they wouldn't feel this way. If I were thin, they'd love me.

Being fat was my friend. As much as I wanted it to go away, I needed it to stay. The hard part was admitting it. For as long as I could remember, I had believed that only people who lacked will power were fat. Only people who were keen on making themselves miserable were fat. Only tortured souls were fat. After reading Susie Orbach's *Fat Is a Feminist Issue*, it occured to me that my struggle with weight might be an indication of emotional issues that, although they were being expressed through food, had little to do with it. Although I wanted to believe that, it sounded *too* good; what if it was a rationalization that would help me remain fat for the rest of my life? What if I discovered that my fat was helping me so much I couldn't let it go?

But I soon realized that the choice was not between remaining fat and getting thin; it was a choice between movement and stasis. One choice required that I shift my self-image from thinking I was tortured and flawed to believing that I was healthy and rational. The other choice asked nothing of me. I didn't have to change, didn't have to risk, didn't have to question societal values and beliefs. The other choice didn't require that I get thin only that I keep wanting to get thin. It allowed me to remain consumed with self-hatred and doubt. The other choice asked nothing of me, the way Shylock asked nothing of Antonio. Except a pound of flesh.

The risk in breaking free is the risk in believing in yourself enough to say, 'Okay. It's true. I've spent all these years dieting and being unhappy about my weight. And although it seems almost absurd to think that I would purposefully not lose weight (it's been such a battle and I've wanted to lose weight so much), I am willing to consider that possibility.'

Compulsive eaters are afraid of themselves. They're afraid because they think that how they eat is at cross purposes with what they want. They focus exclusively on the pain of not being thin, and when I suggest that there is a side to their eating that is rational and helpful, they are suspicious.

Last night in a workshop, someone said, 'At the end of each day, I go through all my experiences and dismiss most of them because I am aware of how different they would be if I were thinner. If I've had a pleasant encounter with someone, I think, "They didn't really mean that, I'm not thin enough to be attractive or competent or empathetic." But if it was a painful meeting, I think, "If I were thin, it would have been different. They wouldn't have done or said or felt that way." It's very sad.'

Yes, it is.

But it is also serving a purpose. It is also helpful in some way that is unacknowledged. In dealing with behaviour that seems neurotic and self-defeating, we have choices. One is to believe we *are* neurotic and self-defeating. Another, the one I choose, is to believe that what looks neurotic and self-defeating, when examined, will reveal behaviour that makes perfect sense given the context in which it occurs.

A close friend of mine is, in her words, 'battling with seven pounds.' When I visited her yesterday she said, 'I don't know who I am when I look in the mirror. I don't know this body, it's so big. My clothes are too tight, I feel ashamed to see people I know or meet people I don't know.'

She talked about Mitchell, the man from whom she had just separated: 'He thought my stomach and legs were too big. He didn't want me to eat so much. "Lose ten pounds," he said, "and you'd look great." '

One night she was eating a bowl of popcorn when she heard his car in the driveway. Frightened of getting caught, she hid the popcorn under her bed.

Two months have passed since they separated. She gained the seven pounds during their time together and says now, 'I can't seem to take it off. I like eating. Meals are the only thing I have to look forward to each day. But it's not fair – other people eat twice as much as I do and they don't gain weight.'

She met Mitchell at a bar; they went home together, made love, and soon after that were seeing each other exclusively. A 'relationship' had begun. But it was never easy. He was a member of a religious sect that she was not interested in joining, much to his disapproval. His career was foundering; hers was rising. He didn't like her body, couldn't share her intellectual interests, and pressured her to follow 'the path'. Their love began, developed, and, toward the end, was only expressed in bed. 'I won't do that again,' she said. 'I won't choose someone who only accepts part of me. He wanted to live according to his spiritual beliefs and physical image and I couldn't. But I'm so lonely without him.'

What does seven pounds have to do with this?

A lot.

A few months ago, seven pounds would have expressed her rage at Mitchell: 'You either love me for who I am – all of me – or you don't. I don't judge you for your balding head. I don't say "Oh, Mitchell, you're losing your hair. I really would prefer you don't." And I don't want you judging my legs or my thighs.'

Now, seven pounds would say, 'You've finally left him, and I'm going to keep you from jumping into bed again with someone you don't know. I'm going to keep you from falling in love with someone you haven't had time to even like. That last one was too painful to repeat. I'm sorry that you're finding me so hard to deal with, but I'd rather you have a hard time with me than another man.'

Seven pounds would also say, 'You're lonely. You just broke up with someone you loved, you're living alone in a new house, you're doing research and applying for jobs. Food is the only thing you have that tastes good. Let me be here for a while. When you don't need me any longer, you'll lose me. And it won't be a battle.'

'But even if that's true, and it probably is,' my friend said, 'it's still hard to be lonely and in transition *and* feel fat.'

'It is,' I said. 'But if you saw a child crying on the side

of the road, would you go over to her, yell at her, kick her?'

'No,' she said quietly. 'I'd hold her, I'd rock her, I'd stroke her.'

We don't purposely try to make life any harder than it already is.

When it looks as if that's what we are doing, it's time to look again.

I encourage clients to proceed from the assumption that what they are doing, although it seems painful and self-defeating, is helping them in ways that are not obvious. It becomes their work then not to punish or change themselves, but to discover how they might be taking better care of themselves. The focus changes from 'I'm hurting myself' to 'I'm helping myself.' Like moving the dial of a kaleidoscope, the colours remain the same but the pattern completely changes.

When you begin from the assumption that what you are doing is helping you, you are placing trust in your instincts and desire for self-protection. You hold yourself, you rock yourself, you stroke yourself.

Turning the Kaleidoscope

There is a tremendous amount of societal resistance to the idea that being overweight serves a valuable purpose. The pressure to be thin and the glory that being thin promises are accepted as Truth and Reality. But why not challenge that view? Why not question the value of time and money and attention spent on the pursuit of slenderness and consider the startling possibility that we have spent years of our lives and thousands of our dollars attempting to find a solution that was always as close as our own experience – our own need for self-preservation. We are like Dorothy in *The Wizard of Oz*, who says, 'If I ever go looking for my heart's desire again, I don't have to look any further than my own backyard because if it isn't there, I never really lost it.'

The backyard. Let's begin there.

THE THIN YOU/THE FAT YOU: WHICH IS YOU?

When I was at my heaviest, and even now when I imagine myself thinner, the image of who I am when I am thin is the night to the day of my fat self. The thin me doesn't walk, she floats into rooms. She is soft and sexual, warm and compelling. She sparkles. She glitters. She entertains. The thin me is sought after, longed for, adored. She wants nothing that she doesn't or can't have. She is a dancer. She is self-absorbed, apolitical, interested in shopping and gossip and men.

The fat me is rooted to the earth through her legs, like tree trunks. She is self-contained, sufficient, a world unto herself. She is silent. She is asexual. She is a writer. She works for the nuclear freeze, protection of the environment. She is alone. She feels hopelessly and forever ugly.

These images are partially based on experience. When I was fifteen or sixteen years old – and on up to my anorexic years – being thin *was* consuming and self-absorbing. I used my attractiveness as a calling card; I didn't value my inner life because I didn't know I had one.

By the time I was in my late twenties, I was ready to pull myself inward, question appearances, and find meaningful work. I don't think it's a coincidence that I gained fifty-five pounds at that point. I didn't believe I could be thin and serious, thin and professional, thin and honest. My past experience and the images of thin women in advertising and on TV convinced me on an unconscious level that being thin meant beauty, men, and sex.

When I became aware that these images were shaping my behaviour, the awareness of it – the naming, the knowing, the questioning – allowed for change. I realized that somewhere between the two images a human being could exist.

● **Who is the fat you? What does she do? How does she feel? What does she need?**

Write a page or two describing the fat you. Be specific about her clothes, her walk, her posture, her expressions. What does she do with her time? How does she feel about the people around her? Does she have intimate relationships? Is she playful, serious, sexy, tough?

If you want to do this exercise in a group, make a list called 'The Fat Me Is . . . ' and don't censor your immediate responses. Brainstorm together. Be specific, be general. Keep writing until there aren't any more answers.

● **Who is the thin you?**

Now describe a portrait of your thin self, either in paragraph form or on a list. And again, describe this image of yourself in detail. How do people respond to her? What kind of clothes does she wear? How does she behave at a party? What are her needs, her values?

● After you have completed the portraits, compare them. How different are they? Are their needs compatible? Which one best describes you as you want to be? As you know you are?

One woman in a workshop wrote:

The Fat Me Is . . .	The Thin Me Is . . .
a recluse	untiring
hiding	male-identified
angry	self-denying
needy	flirtatious
in pain	sexually excitable
hard worker	
not social	

Her fat self and my fat self are so similar, they could pass for sisters. So are many other women's. Fat is for us associated with being quiet and alone, not having to socialize or make small talk, having permission to be unhappy, saying no . . . *all the time*. Being thin is associated with having energy, being sexual, the centre of attention . . . *all the time*.

If you feel that when you are thinner you won't be able to say no (to sexual advances or favours or requests for time) then losing weight can be threatening. And no matter what you tell yourself about how much you want to be thin, you simply won't eat the way a person who wants to lose weight eats, i.e., when you are hungry and until you're satisfied. If the quantity of food you are eating is taking care of you, allaying your fears, allowing you to feel safe, you won't stop because being thinner looks nicer.

Images and associations of the fat you and thin you are just that – images and associations that might be partially founded in experience. They may once have been true. If, when you were younger, you were frightened at the attention you were getting from boys, you might have discovered that when you gained weight, they didn't bother you. You felt safe and protected. It's possible that you forgot the experience but retained the impression and the behaviour of eating and gaining weight.

Our images and associations are fostered by the media's depiction of thin women. If you are shy and quiet and yearn to be gregarious and effusive, you are a perfect target for the TV characters, and the fashion models that skilfully combine thin women with desirable characteristics in enviable situations. You are led to believe that you will have what they have – social ease, attractive men, a satisfying career – when you look the way they look. When you are thin.

Two very subtle pitfalls are exposed here: One is that you are giving your body a life of its own, a personality of its own, and, conversely, you are not giving yourself enough power. It is you, and not your body, who is shy and you, and not your body, who has the power to open your mouth and talk. True, being thinner may allow a certain degree of self-confidence, which in turn allows social ease. But *not always*. If you are quiet by nature, if you don't like parties, it is unrealistic to expect a sudden and major personality change with a major weight loss.

The second pitfall is related to the first: the division and assignment of certain qualities to 'thinness' and 'fatness,' the black and whiteness of being, for instance, flirtatious or energetic as opposed to being in pain and needy. When you make arbitrary divisions like this, you often end up believing them. You begin believing that if you are thinner you cannot be needy. Accept that as a human being, you are sometimes needy no matter why you look like. If being thinner provides no room for what you are and will continue to be, then why be thinner? Who wants to be energetic and flirtatious *all the time*? The pressure and models of behaviour that these divisions assign to body size allow no contradiction or change. It is possible to be energetic and needy, or flirtatious and in pain. If you are not losing weight because who you are does not fit your image of who you think you need or want to be when you are thinner, it is important to reconcile the division of qualities according to weight. There are no personality requirements for a person who is comfortable with her weight.

You can be quiet or flirtatious or needy now, tomorrow, or next week; you don't have to wait to be thinner to be who it is you think you want to be. The standard response I hear to this in a group is 'Sure, but who will respond to a flirtatious overweight person?' The answer is – *a lot* of people.

When I was at my heaviest, people were attracted to me *when I felt attractive*. It's true, there might have been men who would have been attracted to me had I weighed less, but if I had chosen to spend my life with one of those men, what would have happened, where would he have gone, if I'd gotten ill and lost my hair or if I'd gotten pregnant and gained thirty-five pounds?

Attractiveness lies in the way someone holds himself or herself, in his or her willingness to make contact with you. Glenn Close, in an interview in *W*, said 'A lot of the time, I don't feel pretty at all. I think my face is changeable . . . My looks are in the *movement* [italics mine] of my features, not in the stillness.'

Thin bodies get boring very quickly.

● **Two lists that precisely define the benefits of overweight are:**

1. *Being Fat Enables Me To . . .*
2. *Being Thin Means I Can't . . .*

Take some time, either in a group or alone, to complete these. Your answers will tell you exactly how you are using your weight, what it is expressing for you, how it is taking care of you.

● **Now that you've written a portrait of the thin you and the fat you, write a portrait combining the qualities of both.** Spend at least thirty minutes thinking about and then writing an integrated and thoughtful description of the qualities you feel are essential to your well-being. Begin to give yourself the feeling that the ability to be effusive or withdrawn or any other mental or emotional state does not exclusively depend on body size.

The same woman who wrote the two lists on page 163 wrote:

> I can be thinner and work hard. I am in pain sometimes no matter what I look like. I can feel like hiding and be reclusive anytime I want. I don't have to be fat to be unsexual and without a lover. I want the freedom to be any of these things whenever I feel them.

● **Make a list of those things you are waiting to get thin to do.** Call it *I Am Waiting To Get Thin To . . . .* This list is usually a long one. Include small things, like wearing a belt or tucking in a shirt or eating a chocolate chip cookie in public. And bigger things, like buying clothes you like, looking up an old friend – what are you waiting to get thin to do?

● **After the list is made,** *begin doing two 'thin' things a day.* If you like, they can be the same two things for a few consecutive days, but then switch to other, possibly riskier, activities.

Behave like a person who is comfortable with her body. Watch what happens to your walk and the way you do the dishes, the way you sit, the way you talk. The way you eat.

● **Give the fat you a name and write a dialogue between him/her/it and you.** (Give yourself at least two hours to complete this because it usually takes longer than you'd expect to quiet yourself enough to distinguish your voice from the voice of the fat you.) Speak to this part, ask it what it wants, what it needs, how it is taking care of you.

Tell it how you feel about it. Let yourself speak from your heart. If you are angry, be angry. If you are sad, be sad. But begin to make contact with what you have shunned and disliked for so long: the part of you that eats and eats and eats. The dialogue will help you begin a relationship with him or her. It will help you establish communication between two parts of you that have heretofore been warring. There's a potential friend in that part. Together you would probably make a powerful team.

11
On Judgement and Awareness: Birds Don't Sing in Caves

'If I didn't judge myself, my life would be okay, and if my life was okay, I wouldn't know what to do with myself.'

A Breaking Free workshop participant

'I like looking at myself from the back. I don't have a big stomach in the back.'

A Breaking Free workshop participant

When I ask the participants in Breaking Free workshops to count the judgements they make in a day, they return the following week and tell me they stopped after the first half hour because the number was countless.

We think in judgements, we talk in judgements, we act in judgements. Opinions are judgements, decisions are judgements.

Judgements are necessary in many situations; our day-to-day living necessitates making multiple decisions, and decisions necessitate making judgements about which thing is better, timelier, healthier, more effective. Judgements are necessary for physical and emotional survival.

Where the heart is concerned, negative judgements are counterproductive. When there is judgement, there is hardening and resistance and conflict. When there is judgement, there is pulling and pushing and fighting. When there is judgement, compulsive behaviour will continue.

Eight years ago, my friend Ashley met, fell in love with, and married a man who told her, on their third date, that she was too fat. In the past seven years, Ashley has gained seventy pounds.

Donna, a woman in a Breaking Free workshop, is dating a man who tells her that he would be more attracted to her if she lost twenty pounds. 'When he drops me home after an evening out,' she says, 'I go into the kitchen and stuff myself. It's driving me crazy. Since he told me I should *lose* twenty pounds, I've gained ten. I want him to be attracted to me, I love him, but I can't stand him for telling me I should lose weight.'

When our behaviour is harshly judged – whether by ourselves or by someone else – something very tender in us closes down. It's like putting your arms over your head to protect yourself from being hit; you don't want to be vulnerable.

When Donna's lover tells her she needs to lose weight, she withdraws, feeling that his perceptions leave no room for paradox. Although she realizes she is overweight according to the cultural ideal, she also feels fragile: a child-woman who has doubts, uses food to defend herself, to keep people away. She stops trusting him because she feels that if she got lost and forgot where she was going, he wouldn't point her in a direction that led home. She senses that he isn't *for* her, that his vision of her is tailored to his dreams, not hers. And so Donna begins protecting herself from him, answering him curtly, shrinking when he touches her.

When fault is found with our behaviour, a struggle immediately begins. When we feel attacked, we fight back.

Donna's lover's judgements reflect *his problems, not hers*. But because she feels self-conscious and vulnerable, Donna takes what he says about her weight as a personal attack. Her emotional survival is at stake – someone has just told her that she is not good enough the way she is – and she fights back. She chooses her weapon strategically, using only the one that will wound her assailant. Fat.

When her lover sees that Donna is gaining – not losing – weight, he is hurt and angry. (Don't his feelings matter? Didn't he tell her he wasn't attracted to her?) Now, *he* feels attacked, and *his* emotional survival is at stake. So he fights back with a weapon he knows will wound his assailant: criticism about her body. They both feel that the other is not listening and doesn't care. They begin to build walls around themselves, instead of bridges to each other. Impenetrable as they seem from the outside, they are crumbling apart on the inside. The loneliness is terrible, even when they are lying next to each other at night. Perhaps it is sharpest there, in the darkness, when the warmth and the cradle of skin upon skin can no longer blend daylight differences.

I don't think there is any way to stop judging, nor should there be, but I do think we need to be more *aware* of the judgement process. We can work on dis-identifying ourselves from our judgements. Just because we form an opinion about ourselves, or anyone else, doesn't mean it is true. In the same way, we can work on dis-identifying ourselves with other people's opinions about us. Just because someone thinks we are unattractive doesn't mean we are.

If, for instance, someone accused me of being a distracted listener, it would not shove me into a storm of self-doubt. I know that most of the time I am a good listener. I know because I've been told that again and again, and because I feel that the quality of attention I give to people is focused and deep. Because I wouldn't

have to defend my self-worth, I could direct my attention to the person making the remark. I could ask them
if they were hurt about something I did. I could inquire
about what I said – or didn't say – that caused them to
comment on my listening ability. I could focus on what
they were expressing about *themselves* when they used
the smokescreen of a judgement about *me*.

Behind every 'you' statement is an 'I' statement.

'You are a distracted listener' would probably get
translated into 'I need more of your attention.'

'You would be more attractive if you lost twenty
pounds' could be translated into 'I'm frightened about
getting too close to you.'

Ashley's husband has been kicking and screaming for
the entire eight years of their relationship. First he
didn't want to be monogamous; then he didn't want to
live with her; then he didn't want to get married; now he
doesn't want to have children. His pattern has been
similar with other (thinner) women in his life. He is
frightened of intimacy. Sometimes he admits that. But
most of the time he tells Ashley that he withholds his
affection because of her weight (this despite the fact
that their sexual relationship is satisfying to both of
them).

The man is afraid. So are most of us. Love songs don't
prepare us; nothing, no one prepares us for what can be
the stark terror of living with another human being on a
face to face basis with no masks allowed. All that you
never wanted anyone to see – your fears, your confusion,
your needs – is seen. If both of you are willing to tolerate
the discomfort of being revealed, you can use it to bring
you closer, all the while knowing that there are no
guarantees; the person you love could leave. Or die.

When Ashley's husband says 'You're fat' instead of
'I'm frightened,' he absolves himself from the task of

looking deeper to the centre of his own self. He puts the responsibility for his limitations on her; he says 'It's your fault; *you* make it better.' Ashley may or may not believe him. If she does, if she actually believes that he would love her more if she were thinner, the result will be an endlessly unsatisfying exchange. She will be angry because he doesn't love her for *her*; he will be angry because she doesn't lose weight; and because neither of them will be addressing the root of the problem, they will continue to hammer at each other until the relationship breaks.

Patti came to a Breaking Free workshop after twenty years of trying to lose weight. 'My husband,' she said, 'does not like fat women and is constantly telling me that our sex life would be a lot better if I lost weight.' During the course of two eight-week workshops, Patti lost thirty-five pounds. And her husband didn't like it. Suddenly, he had the woman of his dreams and couldn't wake up. They began fighting, sleeping in different rooms. She was confused and enraged ('This is what I've been killing myself over for twenty years?'); he was bitter and resentful ('You've changed,' he said, 'you're not as nice anymore'). They are now seeing a marriage counsellor, hoping to unravel the twenty years of fear, anger, and resentment that have been funneled into, and ignored because of, Patti's 'weight problem.'

Our ability to love, to sustain intimacy, depends on our willingness to push ourselves, gently, through our discomfort and our fears. When we come to walls in ourselves, can we scale them? If our legs aren't strong enough to climb, do we get discouraged? Do we blame it on someone else, tell them they're fat? Or do we take a wall-climbing class?

*   *   *

Ashley has gained nine pounds.

Donna is bingeing nightly.

Judgements beget conflict, hardening, rebellion. When there is judgement, compulsive behaviour will continue.

Yesterday I went to an aerobics class. The instructor of the class is five-seven and weighs 120 pounds. She reminds me of a lioness: sleek, lean, ready. She is thin without being skinny, muscular without being masculine.

Before the class began, I walked into the dancewear shop at the gym and met the instructor in the dressing room. As she was trying on a leotard, she said, 'I am really fat today.' The saleswoman said, 'You? Fat? Aw, come on . . . ' The instructor said, 'I *am*. Look at this –' and she pinched a micromillimetre of flesh at her waist.

I walked back into the exercise room and looked at my body in the mirror. My thighs pyramided their way down to the floor, my waist was thick, my arms were flabby. I dragged my way through the class, and when I got home I walked straight to the refrigerator.

A judgement is a continuous, high-pitched, silent scream. It hurts to listen to it. First you try covering your ears. Then you try leaving the room. Soon you become frantic; you'll do anything to make the shrieking in your head stop.

Eating makes it stop. Eating takes your attention away from the shrill and focuses it on the taste. Eating provides relief from whatever you are judging yourself about, until you start judging yourself for eating. Eating makes it stop until eating makes it start. So eating doesn't make it stop.

Nothing will stop a judgement but the awareness that it is a judgement. You can't fight – and win – against a judgement. It is like pruning a plant, only to have it grow back wider and bushier. When I tell myself that I am fat, *my response is to eat more, not less*.

Judgements evoke a set of feelings, impressions, and beliefs to which we react. It is what we *infer* from judgements that sets up spiralling down into self-doubt and worthlessness. I can't say 'Geneen, your legs are getting a little large; why don't you lose some weight?' without evoking an onslaught of feelings associated with being fat, and it is to these feelings that I react when I walk straight to the refrigerator. These feelings are the silent scream. The voice that says 'You are fat. You are ugly. You are worthless.' It is so painful that I want to vanquish it, get back at it.

We want to be seen and treated as whole human beings. We want to be valued for the parts of us that are not visible when we walk down a street. And with good reason. Those parts – our feelings, our ability to give, receive, compromise, change, our intelligence – take time and effort to develop and deepen. Without them, we are like Easter eggs, brightly coloured but without our centres. When someone tells us, or we tell ourselves, that what really matters is the pattern on the shell and how it looks in the basket with the fake green grass, we feel devalued, unseen. And then we react by doing, being, saying the opposite of whatever we are being judged about.

The heart closes down when confronted with ultimatums, and judgements are, in one form or another, ultimatums. 'If you lose weight, I'd be more attracted to you' is a code version of 'Until you lose weight, I won't give you my full measure of love.' No one can hear that without reacting.

We are always changing; that much is certain. But we cannot change for someone else. We cannot lose weight or become Tibetan Buddhists unless the direction and purpose of that change meshes with our own convictions and dreams and unless we already feel accepted and loved by the person who is asking. Even then, the change is for us. We change for ourselves; we change to come closer and closer to those glimpses, those flashes of who we know we could become if we allowed ourselves to unfold. We change because we have to change, because when we don't, we become stultified, stratified, rock-hard.

Judgements do not lead to change.

Change happens the way a plant grows: slowly, without force, and with the essential nutrients of love and patience and a willingness to remain constant through periods of stasis.

If change is what you want, you need to learn a gentler way of dealing with yourself and others.

Awareness, in contrast to judgement, is the quality of attention that is spacious and light. Awareness is attention that observes what you are doing without pushing you in a particular direction.

Awareness is a voice that notices. Just notices. When you walk into the house and are not hungry and head for the refrigerator, awareness is the voice that says, 'My heart is racing, my hand is in the refrigerator. The food is coming up to my mouth. Now chewing, now swallowing, bringing the food up to my mouth again. Stomach in knots. Cold food. Can't taste it. More food. Still can't taste it . . . what's going on?'

The judging voice says, 'I can't believe you're doing this again! What's *the matter* with you? You will never learn, will you? Here you go, shoving food into your mouth, look at you, you're disgusting. You said you were going to watch what you ate, and now you are doing this. You're just going to keep getting fatter and fatter; soon you'll be wearing nothing but muu-muus.'

The judging voice bullies you into a corner. It pushes you until another voice, the voice of rebellion, pushes back: 'I can do this if I want to; it's *my* body. I've had a hard day. Big deal if I have to wear muu-muus for the rest of my life. I want to eat and I don't care.'

Awareness poses no fight, no scream, no ultimatum. Awareness is the crux of breaking free from compulsive behaviour because as soon as you are aware that you are being compulsive, you are no longer being compulsive.

Compulsive behaviour, by definition, is behaviour that is automatic, unthinking; we engage in it when we want to *be* automatic and unthinking. When we want to numb ourselves, knock ourselves out, when we want to leave ourselves, we turn to food or alcohol or drugs. Therein lies the value of compulsion: removal from discomfort. And therein lies its tragic flaw: you cannot remove yourself from discomfort without also removing yourself from a large portion of your life.

We don't need tricks to help us lose weight. We don't need diets or special foods. We need to decide whether we want to remove ourselves from our lives or whether we want to participate in them. Awareness is the process of joining yourself, of keeping yourself company while you live.

Awareness and compulsion cannot possibly exist together in the same moment. When you turn on a light, it is no longer dark. No matter how compulsive you are, no matter if you've been bingeing for thirty years or thirty minutes, as soon as you are aware that you are bingeing, it is no longer a binge.

For me, the most frightening aspect of compulsive eating was the feeling of being possessed. When I binged, it was as if a demonic spirit entered my body and took control. My movements were wooden, my will dissolved. I felt hypnotized, in a trance. Everything that had been important to me before the binge became irrelevant. My need for food was so urgent that if anyone stood in my way, I wanted to get rid of them.

Later, when I'd stopped eating, my posture relaxed, my eyes lost their glassiness, my relationships became important again. As glad as I was to have myself back, I was frightened. My personalities were so disjointed that I began to wonder if I was insane.

Compulsive behaviour is marked by an awful absence of self. It's as if you had left town, a storm destroyed your house, and you returned in time to survey, and be horrified by, the damage. Fearing that another storm might unleash its fury at any moment, you catapult yourself into an inflexible and strenuous dietary regime. Given the extensive havoc of a binge, it is understandable that the idea of using awareness to treat compulsive eating seems like trying to catch a wild elephant with a mousetrap.

But if compulsion is marked by the absence of self, awareness is marked by the steady, unobtrusive presence of self. And it is precisely this difference that changes the entire nature of compulsive behaviour. When you are watching what you are doing, you simply will not behave in the same way as when you are not watching (i.e., judging yourself, numbing yourself). Awareness works at the root level of compulsion by defusing the momentum of your actions. If you want to knock yourself out but are aware that you want to knock yourself out, you have already brought yourself back. If you are eating and saying to yourself, 'I can't believe you are doing this; you're disgusting,' but are aware that you are saying this, you have already removed yourself from the trap of reacting to the judgement.

Awareness lends perspective to an otherwise unbearably smack-up-against-it situation. You are always more powerful than the food on your table and your judgements about your body; awareness brings that realization home.

But suppose you're aware that you want to knock yourself out and you decide to do it anyway. Being aware will still change your attitude about what you're doing. You will not feel that you've come back into town after a storm. You will not feel victimized and at the mercy of desires raging inside you. You will feel that you made a choice and that the choice was to eat when you weren't hungry. You're allowed. (Everyone eats compulsively. The difference between those who come to workshops for it and those who don't is that the latter eat and go on with their day; the former eat and let it ruin their day. The difference is not in the action, it's in the attitude *about* the action.) When you make a conscious decision to eat compulsively, you give yourself the chance to explore the terrain of compulsion – how it feels, whether you enjoy it, whether you want to do it again – and to learn for the next time.

Awareness places no more value on abstinence than on indulgence. Awareness asks that if you indulge, you notice what it feels like and whether you indeed experience the pleasure you hoped for.

Awareness assumes that you want to learn, grow, spread your wings, fly. And that you need to practice in large, open spaces. Awareness assumes that, at the beginning, you will trip and fall, but if you don't get discouraged, if you keep learning from each fall, you will learn how to fly.

Negative judgement assumes that you do not have the desire or sufficient motivation to get off the ground. It assumes that given large spaces, you will grovel, you will waste time, you will crumple.

Doesn't it know that wild elephants walk softly in open fields?

Practising in Large Spaces

● **Count the judgements you make in a day.** Begin with the moment you open your eyes. What is the first opinion you have? The second? As you go through the day, notice how often you make judgements about how much you see – people's clothes, their walks, their expressions. Your clothes, your walk, your expressions. You probably have an opinion about *everything*, and you will probably continue to have an opinion about everything. But your opinions are just opinions; they are not unequivocal truth. You can either notice that they come and they go and not take them so seriously, or you can *believe* each one of them and shape your actions accordingly. Which is more comfortable?

● **Every time you judge something or someone, tag the judgement with 'The sky is blue'.*** If you think someone has behaved selfishly, end the thought with 'the sky is blue.' 'I can't believe how large my thighs are. The sky is blue. That car is ugly. The sky is blue. She really shouldn't wear a bikini. The sky is blue. I am never going to stop eating; this problem is hopeless. The sky is blue.'

The purpose of adding a toneless statement to a judgement is that it neutralizes its charge. It makes you very aware that you are, in fact, judging and that it is not necessary to get caught up in the process.

● **Pay very close attention to the physical sensations of being judged.** They are most obvious when the

* Thank you, Joseph Goldstein, for this helpful exercise.

judgement is external, when someone else is comment-ing on what you've said or done or eaten. What happens in your stomach? In your chest?

● **Pay close attention to the emotional sensations of being judged.** What is your first thought or feeling after you hear what someone says? Do you feel receptive or loving to the person judging you? Do you want to change your behaviour to accommodate him or her? How do you now feel about yourself? Do you want to eat?

● **Think of a friend by whom you feel loved and accepted.** What happens when you do something she doesn't like? How does she communicate her dissatisfac-tion? Does she tell you she'll stop loving you if you don't change? Does she threaten you, or does she communi-cate in a way that allows you to consider your actions, her feelings, and your reaction to both? Do you feel backed into a corner or do you feel the freedom to move?

● **Make a list of the times you've changed as a result of either judging yourself or being judged by someone else.**

● **Think about the times in your life you've made long-lasting changes.** Write down three major attitudinal or behavioural changes you've made in the past ten years and describe the situations in which they occurred: the people around you, whether or not you were working, what you were doing, feeling, thinking. Did the changes occur when you were feeling cared for and safe or did they come about because you felt threatened?

Can you be specific about the process of change? Do you judge yourself for not being a certain way and then attempt to change your behaviour? Does long-lasting change come from fear of not being good – or of being a

bad person – or does it come from a desire to express
your intuitive sense of your capabilities?

● **Divide a piece of paper in two parts. On the left
side, write 'Judgement' and on the right side, write
'Counterjudgement'.** Pick a judgement that you frequently make about yourself. Write it under the judgement heading. Now, counter that judgement with a
response. For instance, if you wrote 'My hips are huge,'
what is your immediate response? If it's 'Yes, they are,'
then write that down. Now, write the judgement again:
'My hips are huge,' and answer it again: 'Well, they
aren't *that* huge' or, 'They're so huge that no one likes
me because of them.' Keep writing until the counterjudgement is *at least neutral*.

Do this once a day for ten days. Eventually you will
discover that a judgement is relative, subjective, and a
product of the moment. Learn how to work with your
judgements so that you don't continually live in reaction to them.

● **Imagine that your judging voice has a name.**
What would it be? Now, imagine that you are talking
with it. Ask what it wants, what it is afraid of. Ask how
it is trying to help you. Every time you notice that you
are judging yourself, speak to it by name. Say, 'Hi, ——,
you're back. What's up?' Enter into a dialogue with
yourself, establish open and friendly communication
with voices that seem to be at cross-purposes. I think
you'll find that they all want the same thing – they want
you to be happy – but are not sure how best to go about
it. You need to teach them.

● **When someone is judging you, tell him or her to
stop.** This situation arises again and again in Breaking
Free workshops. The participants leave the workshop

excited with the possibility of treating themselves and food with respect. During the week a friend or an acquaintance invariably comments on what someone is eating. If it's chocolate cake, shouldn't she be eating carrots instead? Most of my clients greet such a comment with silence or a murmur of assent, and go right on to finish the chocolate cake.

Other people's judgements are most often a reflection of *their* inability to accept *themselves*, not an indication of your shortcomings. People judge others about that which they judge in themselves; if they are uncomfortable with their weight, they are going to be very aware of your weight. If they are afraid to eat chocolate cake, they will be disturbed when they see you eating it because it will bring up their own fear and their own desire to do what you are doing. They will try to push away the external cause of their disturbance – you.

Remember that a judgement is only one person's opinion; its reality is subjective and contextual. One person can look at you and marvel at your clear skin; someone else will comment about the blemish on your forehead. Because the judgemental process is insidious and automatic, you will be the object of it from time to time. If you are experimenting with food in a way that is not accepted as *the* way, you will hear more comments than usual. Remind yourself immediately that these people are talking about themselves and not about you. Tag their judgements with 'the sky is blue,' and tell them gently but firmly that their judgements do not help you to change. Then, if you like, give yourself another kind of judgement: a compliment!

● **When you are judging yourself, don't get caught by trying to disprove the judgement or by allowing it to provoke a chain of implications to**

which you then react. I suggest two alternatives:

Ask yourself what is really going on. When I'm feeling fat, it is a reliable indicator that I am disturbed about something less tangible or less familiar. Feeling fat is a mask; it enables me to hide behind a well-worn problem while preventing me from discovering the source of the current and less familiar pain. Next time be more specific. Examine the components of the feeling. When you hear yourself say, 'I'm fat,' ask yourself what you are feeling fat *about* – your work, your children, your friendships, something you did or didn't say. Think of feeling fat as a metaphor that describes just about anything uncomfortable instead of a situation that has to do with, and that you must remedy by altering, your body weight.

The second alternative is to put a frame around judgements as they arise. Every time you feel an 'I'm fat' or an 'I'm worthless' coming on, label it Judgement Number 3,456 and go on with your day. When the next judgement arises, do the same thing. When you reach a million, begin again.

12
On Trust

'Still, for me, the most difficult thing is to be
able to feel that it is a good thing to say, "I'm
worth it." '

A Breaking Free workshop participant

'My big fear is still one of thinking there's
nobody inside, no authentic or original voice.'

A Breaking Free workshop participant

Writing a book, I've discovered, has much in common
with resolving weight issues. You can proceed from the
fear that unless you force yourself to do it, you won't. Or
you can proceed from the belief that you want to do it,
and will, but that doing it may sometimes look like not
doing it. One way is as difficult as the other; both
require perseverance and commitment. The way you
choose depends on how you want to live. You can fear
yourself or you can trust yourself.

I thought I had made a decision. Until recently, when
a friend pointed out that I'd been writing the way I
encourage people not to eat. I'd wake up, I'd shower, I'd
eat breakfast, and I'd sit at my desk. For six hours a day,
six days a week. Then I'd take a dance class, then I'd
lead a workshop, then I'd go to sleep. On Sunday, I'd
take the day off. Twice in six weeks I have been sick;
both illnesses have lasted two weeks. Last Tuesday I
had a lecture to give at a hospital, and on Monday, I
awoke tired and congested. I decided to work on the book
for a few hours and write the lecture in the afternoon. I
tried to put a sentence together. Noun, verb, object. No

words came. I tried again. No words. I sat there for an hour. The tension began rising from my calves. 'I can't do this,' I thought, 'I can't finish the book by April, lead workshops in Santa Cruz, Los Angeles, Boulder, New Orleans, New York, Boston, New Haven, Dallas, *and* keep my relationships alive. I can't.' I felt like a set of bowling pins that had been perfectly aligned until one pin, the pressure of writing a lecture, fell and knocked the rest down with it. 'One wrong move,' I remember someone in a workshop saying, 'one bit of the wrong food and the day is shot. I eat everything in sight.' One pin.

'What's more important?' my friend asked, 'getting the book done or your life while you are writing it?'

'What's more important,' I ask the members of a workshop, 'losing weight or your feelings about yourself while you are losing it?'

'That's an unfair question,' I tell my friend. 'It's just a few more months of this pressure. After that, I'll be able to relax.'

Like studying for final exams, I say. You put all your energy into studying and then it's over. This is a heightened time, I say.

'Just one more diet,' the members of the Breaking Free workshop say. 'We'll lose the weight, it'll take a month, maybe two, and then we'll start eating what we want and working on the emotional issues.'

Like studying for final exams? I ask. Yes, they say, once we lose the weight, we can feel good enough about ourselves to concentrate on other things. This is a special time, they say.

'What would happen if you relaxed *now*?' my friend asks. 'If you let yourself have some flexibility in your writing schedule, what would happen?'

I can't, I say.

I either write the book according to a schedule that allows no room for mood shifts or energy levels or inspiration or the book will not get done.

'What would happen if you started now?' I ask the participants. 'If you let yourself eat anything you wanted, what would happen?'

We can't, they say.

We either lose weight according to a diet that allows no room for mood shifts or specific cravings or body wisdom or we won't lose the weight.

'Why?' my friend asks.

'Why?' I ask them.

Because, we say.

Our hunger is deep, it is old. Our hunger is wild. Unless we shackle it, cage it, silence it, it will devour us, and we, in turn, will devour the world.

The hunger that demands release. The hunger that roams in the caves of our bodies. The hunger, not just for food, but also for intimacy, for comfort, for sex, for satisfying work, for setting limits, for self-expression. The hunger that has never been allowed to speak. The hunger that was squelched years ago, before we could fight back, before we could wonder why. The messages we received about ourselves and our bodies, about our hungers: that we were intrusive, that we demanded too much, that if we ate what we wanted, we'd be fat, sick, unhealthy. And if we did what we wanted, we'd do nothing, be worthless, destroy ourselves.

If we won't allow ourselves a cookie, or if we can't stop after bags of cookies, we are the same. We are women afraid of ourselves. We are women being eaten alive with hunger.

The women in my groups invariably describe their illnesses, no matter how serious, as 'okay because I can't eat.' Lenore told her group that when her grandmother was dying of cancer, her mother remarked on how 'beautifully thin' she was getting and on how 'she never looked better.' Lenore said, 'My grandmother was losing her hair, she was in horrible pain, but she was thin. And my mother was envious.'

It is ironic that in our culture women have come to equate hunger with that which harms us instead of that which enlivens us. We embrace anything that helps us lose our appetites. Even death.

Trusting ourselves means being willing to hunger. For food, for intimacy, for comfort, for self-expression.

It is the denial, not the acknowledgement, of hunger that destroys us.

We are all hungry for something.

In a workshop, Abby said, 'When will this hunger end? Every week I go shopping for precious forbidden food. And sometimes it stays in my house – I've had a gallon of ice cream there now for a week – and sometimes I eat it all. But how do I know I won't keep eating and eating, how do I know that eventually I'll lose weight, how do I *know*?'

She *doesn't* know. That's the risk. It could be that she'll never stop eating, that she'll eat until she gains 200 pounds, that she will eat until she can't fit into a door, a chair, a bus. That's the risk she takes when she begins trusting herself – that she will discover that she can't make her own decisions, that she must be told what to do, say, wear, and eat – otherwise she will destroy herself. The risk is discovering that what she *already believes* about herself is true: She is another in the long line of devouring women.

When I started eating without dieting I was already the heaviest I had ever been, and still I ate brownies, cookies, ice cream in front of family and friends. No one understood what I was doing; at times, I wasn't sure *I* understood. I had nothing to show for my belief that eating was taking care of me. I was fat, getting fatter; I wasn't working, didn't have money or a place to live, didn't know what I wanted to do. My worst fears about myself were coming true; I wanted to go on a diet, grab onto structure, have someone tell me what to do. But something stronger than fear pulled me through: the need to know, to trust. The only thing stronger than fear was the desire not to live in fear for the rest of my life.

The most difficult part, the part during which I was fat and eating ice cream, lasted a year. Now, when people come into a workshop and after two weeks say, 'I can't do this, I'm too frightened,' I recognize their terror. And I urge them to continue. Fear is not a sign that you should stop. Fearing yourself does not mean you cannot trust yourself. You can – and need – to go gently, be tolerant and patient with yourself, but you can – and need – to examine your fear, notice whose voices it contains, check it against reality. You've already spent too many years being afraid.

Society teaches us to mistrust ourselves. Society tells us that we've got to diet to lose weight. Society warns us to be afraid of ourselves. This is new territory; you've got to be willing to be a trailblazer.

You've got to want to trust yourself more than you want to be thin. Because there are no guarantees. This isn't a diet; this is life. I can't promise you that if you listen to yourself you will lose ten pounds in two weeks. You might discover that you *don't want to lose weight right now*. And if you don't want to lose weight right now, you won't, whether you diet or not. If you know that you don't want to lose weight, you don't have to pretend that you're trying and then punish yourself when you fail. Trusting yourself means being willing to discover the truth about yourself. And to value the process of discovering that truth.

Can I trust myself?

I think back to Big Sur. I was living in an eight-by-ten cabin with no hot water, no shower, no bathroom. The sun was sharp and hot, the mountains jagged and overpowering. I didn't know what to do or how to make sense of my life. I read Sylvia Plath that summer, her poems and her letters home. I lay on the bed, the softness of my grandmother's quilt underneath me, the open door, the violet and gold pansies rustling in the wind. I could swallow a bottle of bleach, I thought, drive my car off the mountain. I didn't know that summer whether I wanted to live.

I know now.

That's one thing I can trust.

I can trust that I will not kill myself.

What else? What else can I trust?

I can trust that I want to trust myself and that sometimes I will frighten myself. I can trust that I want to keep living on the edge of what is comfortable for me and that I am willing to examine, even when it is painful, why I do what I do and try to discover another way. I can trust that I will listen. I can trust that I like chocolate. I can trust that I am doing the best I can at the moment. I can trust that my hunger is not bottomless. I can trust that I like to dance. I can trust that I will get angry and afraid and impatient and overwhelmed and continue to do what I am angry and afraid and impatient and overwhelmed about doing. I can trust that the anger and fear and impatience and overwhelmingness will end.

I used to think my hunger was so deep and so old that

if I ever listened to it, if I ever let myself eat what I wanted, I would begin in my kitchen and then I would make my way through Santa Cruz, San Francisco, California, Oregon, the Midwest, and eastward. Then I ate a tuna fish sandwich. And got full.

I used to think my hunger was so wild that if I ever listened to it, if I ever let myself do what I wanted, I would never work. I would sleep until one in the afternoon, I'd read magazines, I'd go out to lunch, I'd winter in Greece and summer in Maine.

Then I wrote a book.

And now I'm writing another.

Touching Bottom

Sometimes, when I ache from loneliness or sadness and want to be held, I am afraid that if anyone came near, I would engulf them, walk them into my skin. I don't like seeing myself so needy, and I don't like making myself as vulnerable as I do when I ask. I'm ashamed of needing, ashamed of myself for being so weak. So I hide the need behind silence or smiles. I tell myself I can deal with it alone. I tell myself it will go away. And it never does. And then I begin thinking that no one likes me for me, that if they really knew the depth of my hunger they would go away. I begin resenting how much I listen to other people talk about *their* hungers. I withdraw, and in that withdrawal, I create more of the loneliness I am aching to ease.

The same is true of food hunger. If I don't trust myself to stop eating a certain food, if I don't trust myself to take what satisfies me without devouring the rest of it, then I won't eat that food. But the hunger for it doesn't go away; it stays, and I make it worse by compounding it with fear. What could have been a simple, straightforward act of satisfying my hunger turns into a series of push-pull behaviours (I can't/I want it/I can't/I want it/I can't/I'll have it anyway) that eventually results in a binge.

If you watch carefully, you will notice a similar dynamic involved with many hungers: the recognition of it, the shame about it, the reluctance to satisfy it, the persistence of that hunger, the fear that it is unending, the resentment that no one is perceiving and satisfying your hunger. And so you make the transition from a person who feels hungry to a person who is victimized by that hunger.

When I finally come out and ask to be held, it usually takes fifteen minutes for the ache to subside. Sometimes it takes an hour.

When I finally decide to eat what I want, I get full on one portion. Sometimes two.

The hard part is deciding to ask, to reach, to satisfy. When I don't ask, I am acting out of the belief that something is wrong with me because I need. When I do ask, I am acting out of the belief that I am a good enough human being, and although at the moment my need and fear of needing seem to be pulling me down into the centre of space, I am more than just that need.

It isn't easy to ask. Each time, I pull myself out of the maelstrom of need, form the words, and force myself to say them. Once the words have been spoken, the worst part is over. If whoever I ask says no, I'm disappointed, sometimes hurt, but I'm *never* devastated. My isolation and fear of endless need have already been broken by the act of asking.

Eating what you want also takes courage. You have to believe your hunger will end; you have to believe that you are a good enough human being to have what you want. Eating what you want is a way of telling yourself that you believe in yourself, that you needn't be afraid. Eating what pleases you is part of the complex need to trust yourself, to trust that what you want will satisfy – not destroy – you.

● **Here are some questions for you to ask yourself.** Sit quietly with them; take half an hour and respond to them as truthfully as you can.

What are you hungry for?

How do you feel about needing?

How do you feel when other people need something from you?

Think back on a time when you were very hungry for something – a touch, a particular food – and then got it. How much did it take to satisfy you?

Have you ever had an unending hunger?

Are your ideas about how much it takes to satisfy you different from the reality of how much it takes?

● **Write a page on all the things you can trust about yourself**, the little things (for example, that you like, have always liked, and will always like dried apricots), the big things (for example, that you listen when a friend needs you), the bigger things (for example, that you want to live, grow, become yourself – or that you don't). What makes someone a trustworthy person? Do you fit that description?

● **Every day for one week, ask someone for something.** There is nothing to be ashamed of; we are all hungry for something. Those who seem as if they aren't, are. They are either hiding it well or they aren't needy at that moment. Be discriminating about whom you ask and what you ask for. Start small, with close friends or family. Pay attention to the inner process of asking – the fear, the reluctance, the relief. How do you feel about yourself when you ask?

Practice asking. Make an agreement with a good friend that you are free to ask each other for anything but that both of you are also free to say no. If you haven't asked for anything in a week's time, ask. Even if it's for something small, like talking on the phone for five minutes when you know your friend doesn't like the phone.

When you ask, the very worst that could happen is that someone will say no. And that's painful. But something takes place in the asking that lasts longer even than pain: a confirmation of your self-worth. When you ask, you have decided that you are good enough to ask.

We can trust that hungers change from day to day. We need and then we don't. We give and then we can't. We are constantly involved in changing roles, in being the giver, then the receiver, then the giver again. We can trust that hungers end, that they only *seem* unending when we are in the middle of them and that they only *become* unending when we refuse to acknowledge them.

Ramona came into a Breaking Free workshop saying that she could never eat what she wanted because, if she did, she'd never stop. 'I'm so hungry,' she said, 'from all those years of dieting that I want to eat the world. And not only that – I can.'

I asked her, 'What is the food you'd get fat on, what is it that you could eat and eat and eat and never stop until you had devoured the world?'

'German chocolate cake,' she said, 'from Gayle's Bakery.' I told her to go out to Gayle's and buy German chocolate cake. And then eat it.

She came back the next week and told us, 'I sat down

at the table with the entire cake. I was going to eat the whole thing. Then I ate one big piece. And for some reason, that was enough.'

13

On Courting and
Befriending and
Forgiving Yourself

'If I'm not special to anyone, does that mean
I'm nobody special?'

A Breaking Free workshop participant

The most painful part of compulsive eating is not incurred by the binges you go on or the weight you gain or how you look in a bathing suit. The most powerful part isn't even in the looks you get, the comments that are made about your body. The most painful part is how you translate those events, what you think they reveal about the person you are.

'Being fat is the ultimate failure,' I once wrote in my journal. 'No matter what else I am, if I am fat, the fatness negates it all.'

That means that when I am fat, my words don't matter, my love doesn't matter, my laugh doesn't matter. When I am fat, *nothing matters.*

When my editor read the first draft of *Feeding the Hungry Heart*, she kept crossing out 'self-hatred' and substituting 'self-negation.' 'Self-hatred sounds too strong,' she said. 'No,' I said, 'It's not strong enough.'

The loathing that a person who is or feels fat directs at herself is consuming, it is furious, it destroys everything in its path. I used to imagine taking knives to my body, slicing the flesh and leaving myself thin. Bleeding, but thin. I felt as if I were suffocating in my fat, and I couldn't stand it. What I also couldn't stand was the feeling that I was wasting myself, that all my potential as a writer, teacher, friend, lover, dancer was buried under layers and layers of fat. I couldn't stand dreaming about what I would do if only I were thin, and then staying fat. I wanted to rip myself apart, bone by bone.

There *isn't* a word strong enough to describe what feeling fat can do to a woman.

They come to Breaking Free workshops and they pummel themselves, step on themselves, grind themselves. They come thinking that they hate themselves because they are fat. And they come expecting, hoping, praying that I will have an answer, that I will tell them how to be thin. When I say the unthinkable – that they must begin liking themselves the way they are at this very moment – without losing one pound – they look at me as if I've taken leave of my senses.

'You mean I have to like *this*?' they say, pointing to their bodies.

'That's you,' I say, 'that's not just your body, that's *you*.'

They shake their heads.

'This isn't me,' they say. 'This is my fat. I'm *inside* the fat. I have to get *rid* of the fat to get to myself.'

'That's you,' I say. 'You *can't* get rid of yourself; you can only *accept* yourself.'

'After I lose the weight,' they say, 'then I can like myself.'

'If you can't like yourself now,' I say, 'you won't like yourself then, either.'

They don't buy that. It is inconceivable that they could like this lump of fat, this plodding, lumbering, spineless human being.

Today is February twenty-eighth. The book is due on April first. And I feel fat. For months I've been sitting at this desk and writing, getting up from this desk and eating. Little bites at a time, a carrot, a cookie, a pretzel. I've been eating to crunch down on something, to break the stillness, not because I'm hungry. My clothes feel a little tighter; I've probably gained a pound, maybe two. But it doesn't matter. I feel fat. And when I feel fat, nothing is right.

I talk to Sara about it. She tells me she loves me. She tells me that I don't look as if I've gained weight. 'But,' she says, 'even if you have, it's not the end of the world. You are still who you are; five pounds here or there makes no difference.'

I talk to my mother. She tells me to eat a poached egg in the morning, a salad in the afternoon, and a piece of fish and vegetable for dinner. 'Don't tell me what to eat, Mom,' I say, 'that's not what I need to hear.' So she tells me that when the book is done, the weight will 'slip away.'

I feel fat. And when I feel fat, my vision becomes skewed. My perception of reality completely changes: I see only fat or thin. I compare myself to every slender woman in the grocery store, the bank, the gas station. I stare at bodies in my dance class and wonder what they eat and how their thighs can stay so slender. My sense of myself is vague; I'm not sure who I am. Feelings and words and actions lose their crispness, their definition. I move slowly, as in a stupor. I apologize for myself over and over. At five pounds, twenty pounds, or forty pounds overweight, I feel the same: When I am fat, it is always night.

I think about faces as I sit here, writing. I think about Luna last Tuesday night, her tears, her anger: 'I can't stop hating myself. I can't. I know that it will be easier to like myself when I am thin.'

I look down at my own body and feel that I am beginning to sink. If I get submerged in this self-hate after five years of working on this programme, after writing books and leading workshops and giving lectures, how difficult it must be for someone coming into a group for the first time. Luna's face, her tears.

'How can I befriend myself when I look like this?' she says. 'And if I start liking myself when I'm overweight, what will motivate me to get thinner?'

We're back to the beginning.

What comes first?

Liking yourself and therefore wanting to care for yourself (with food, in relationships) or losing weight and liking yourself?

I say liking yourself comes first.

And I say it because for seventeen years of my life I loathed myself because I wasn't thin. Except that during many of those years, I *was* thin. And it made no difference.

And I say it because they come to Breaking Free workshops with the same stories: Luna has already been thin. Did she like herself any more? 'No,' she says. 'Not really.'

How, then? How do we like this spineless, plodding, lump of fat? How do we like what we hate? How?

I used to dream about the kind of body I'd have when I grew up. It would be very tall and very thin. Long lanky legs, little breasts. My hair would be thick and curly, my eyes dark and mysterious.

Then I grew up. And I couldn't get used to the fact that this was it: These legs weren't growing any longer, this hair wasn't getting any thicker, these eyes weren't getting any darker. All those years of lying under my cranberry quilted bedspread in my pink and white bedroom dreaming about what I would look like when I grew up, and this was it.

I also used to dream about the kind of man I'd love when I grew up. He would be tall, burly, dark. His face would be angular, he'd have a moustache. His thick black hair would curl gently over his collar. His eyes would be as green as the sea before a storm.

The last time I fell in love, it was with a man who was two inches taller than I. He had freckles all over his fair-skinned body. His hair – what was left of it – was red; it didn't reach far enough to curl over his collar. I think his eyes were blue, but I don't really know. He was so near-sighted that he had to wear his glasses for everything, even making love.

I loved him. I loved him despite, and then because of, his looks.

When he gained five pounds and a paunch tumbled over his pants, I never, not for a moment, stopped loving him.

It's in me, this love. It's in me to love in spite of, and then because of, looks that do not fit my ideal, looks I had no intention of loving.

Can I take this love and direct it to me, my hips, my thighs? Can I love myself with the loyalty and generosity that I show to others?

At the beginning of each Breaking Free workshop group, we do an eyes-closed exercise. Last night I asked the participants to put their hands on an area of their bodies they didn't like. No one moved. After what seemed like a long time, someone placed her hands on her thighs. The rustling of her clothes as she moved inspired someone else to put her hands on her belly. Then another woman put her hands on her breasts. More and more women placed their hands on their hips, their thighs, their faces, their buttocks. I asked them to be gentle with these parts of themselves. Some let their hands rest lightly on their bodies; some massaged themselves. When they opened their eyes, three women were crying:

'It never occurred to me to be *gentle* with my thighs; that makes me so sad.'

'I go around hating my stomach, wishing it would go away. But for a moment, when I touched it, it was just my stomach . . . nothing to hate.'

'My breasts are part of me, they're part of *me*. I spend so much time hating them and all the while I am hating myself.'

We hate our bodies. As if we could force them to change by the sheer intensity of our hatred. We treat ourselves and our bodies as if love destroys and hatred heals.

'I don't want to start liking this fat,' someone said. 'If I do, what will motivate me to lose weight?'

'Nothing,' someone replied, 'nothing.'

I was riding on a bus in San Francisco; a fat woman was sitting in the back, eating quickly and furtively from a mesh sack filled with candy bars, hamburgers, and frankfurters. Within ten minutes, she had eaten three candy bars, a hamburger, and a frankfurter. She didn't seem concerned with getting to a destination; I had the feeling she was sitting on the bus so that she could eat. I wondered if she would ride until her sack was empty. I wondered if she would buy more food, get on another bus. As I stepped off the bus, she was unwrapping another hamburger; the bus doors closed behind me and I stood on the street corner and cried.

When the women in my groups tell me that they are afraid they will keep eating if they begin liking themselves and that they will keep getting fatter and fatter if they don't force themselves to change, I tell them about her. 'Was it love that kept her on the bus?' I ask them. 'Was this a woman who liked herself?'

We have gotten the idea that change results from force and deprivation and that liking ourselves leads to stasis and indolence. We are afraid of accepting ourselves the way we are. We are afraid that we will become women who ride endlessly on buses, eating hamburgers and candy bars from mesh sacks.

Think about friendship: how you feel with a good friend, what you expect in a friend, what you give to a friend, what you hear when I say, 'Befriend yourself.'

It is important, when we are using such hackneyed expressions as 'liking yourself' and 'befriending yourself' to look beyond the image of the cliche and reinvestigate the meaning that the words have for you. If you say that you will not change when you like yourself, ask yourself what that means.

Is it true that you do not change when you are liked?

In addition to hearing the fear that accepting and liking ourselves will lead to complacency, I also hear something else in Breaking Free workshops when I mention liking ourselves: that there isn't enough to like. Asked what is wrong with themselves, the participants in Breaking Free workshops will give long elaborate lists. Asked for what is valuable about themselves, they fall silent.

The feeling of worthlessness is pervasive among compulsive eaters. The feeling is that who they are is bad, unlovable, lazy, selfish, and that they need to hide the truth of themselves behind personas that are kind and giving and happy and bright.

Maybe.

But if they do, so does everyone else.

Backstage at the Kirov is a film about the making of *Swan Lake*. A friend who saw it said, 'Who wants to see the ballerinas' straps fall down and hear the squeaking of their toe shoes and watch the sweat drip off their foreheads? Who wants to know what hard work it is? I want to see the beauty, not the struggle.'

Not me. I struggle. And I want to see the struggle as well as the beauty in others. I struggle, and when I see only grace and beauty in other people, I think something is wrong with me. I think, 'Living comes easy to them; they are naturally graceful, kind, generous, thin. None of those qualities comes easily to me. Something is wrong . . . with me'.

Whenever I glowingly describe a person I have met to Sara, she says, 'They sound wonderful.' Then she pauses and says, 'So what do they struggle with?' Obviously I don't know the answer, but her response immediately puts my canonization of them into perspective. It forces me to remember that everyone struggles with herself – that everyone has bad dreams, that everyone cries and fails miserably and is selfish and lazy and bitchy.

We don't see the struggle of people we admire, the people we respect. We don't see how movies are made, the fights among the performers, the exhaustion at the end of the day. We don't see the sweat of the model standing under hot lights for six hours. We don't see public figures fighting with their spouses. We don't see them waking up in the morning or ill with the flu. We don't see them vomiting or crying or worrying. We see the outcome of their struggle; we see the results of their hard work. We see them well, sparkling, succeeding. We can't look inside them. But we are constantly looking inside ourselves, comparing our insides with their outsides. And it's an unfair comparison.

When *Feeding the Hungry Heart* was published, I got a letter from a college acquaintance who wrote:

[When I discovered that you'd written a book] I felt a lot

of pain . . . I found myself in a fit of rage and invalidation that a contemporary of mine was so much further along the same road I am attempting to travel. I was jealous of the ease with which you seem to fill your groups, jealous of some of your beautiful prose. I also sense that you have let go of the weight issue more than I . . . I have had a lust for recognition . . . and when I see an equal, not someone who's forty years old, but an equal, being more recognized, I feel threatened and start questioning myself.

Her letter arrived in the middle of August. Since July first I had been trying to begin this book. Each day I'd awaken anxious that I couldn't write, and each day the anxiety would get worse. I felt incompetent and blocked and uncreative. I wanted to crawl out of my skin, become someone else; and then I received a letter from someone who wanted what she thought I had.

The glory of others, and the worthlessness of ourselves, are relative. They are usually decided upon *in comparison* with someone whose struggle is not apparent.

When I compare how selfish I know I can be to the apparent generosity of someone else, the gulf between us is immeasurable. But I know I am comparing my darkest hour to their brightest hour, my private face to their public face. My college friend created an image of me from what I had written and compared that image with her own unrealized dreams and the knowledge of her shortcomings. She imagined that my workshops filled effortlessly and that food was no longer an issue in my life. But her *image* of me was not *me*; I was sitting at my desk struggling with words. Sometimes I was using food to ease the pain. I always worry that a workshop will not fill. I was not her perception of me, yet it was upon her perception that she invalidated herself, was jealous and in pain.

Worthlessness is relative. It depends on what you see when you look at someone else and how you compare that to yourself. It depends on your willingness to expand your definition of, and develop a relationship with, yourself.

Beginning a relationship with yourself is like beginning a relationship with anyone else you come to value and love. First comes the courting: discovering each other, playing together, delighting in one another. This is the point at which, for lovers, just being together is enough – gazing into each other's eyes, walking hand in hand, making love in the afternoon.

Most of us have done this with lovers (so we know how) but we've never done it with ourselves. We need this time with ourselves, however, this willingness to get to know ourselves, to discover and then to value what pleases us.

In Breaking Free workshops, the fear of being powerful arises for many women when they begin courting themselves. When they begin valuing themselves the way they are instead of constantly berating and trying to change themselves, they begin feeling stronger and more self-assured. When they begin feeling stronger and more self-assured, they feel a surge of the joy and strength that self-appreciation brings. But then they begin worrying, both because of actual and imagined experience, that if they allowed themselves to be as powerful as they knew they could be, they would alienate friends, lovers, colleagues. Women would feel threatened; men would feel intimidated. So, rather than take that chance, these women drain their personal power (i.e., the ability to say no, to set limits, to ask for what they want) by disliking their bodies, which often translates into disliking themselves. It is impossible to feel self-assured and powerful when, given the chance, you'd slice away flesh and leave yourself bleeding, but leave yourself thin.

Befriending ourselves, taking time to discover what pleases us, and appreciating what and who we already are can represent our first steps toward reclaiming our personal power.

When you befriend yourself, you discover that there's somebody home, and when you've been knocking at the door for years without getting an answer, that's very reassuring.

Making Friends With Our Bodies

We begin with our hips, our breasts, our thighs, our buttocks. And we begin now. There is no reason to wait. It doesn't get easier. If you are looking with critical eyes, you will find flaws in anything: Fat thighs won't be thin; thin thighs will have cellulite. If you are looking with critical eyes, there is no such thing as an acceptable body. Stop waiting for permission to like yourself. No one can give it to you.

● **Pick an area of your body that you dislike.** Put your hands on it, rub it, massage it, be tender with it. So far, you haven't gotten rid of it by wishing or hating it away. Try talking to it. Try asking it what it needs from you. Touch it as you would a bird's breast. Quietly, carefully, softly.

● **Go through your closet and get rid of the clothes that you don't like or that don't fit you.** Especially the tight ones, the ones you have to pour yourself into, the ones that dig into your waist and your thighs and the ones that stand when you sit. *Get rid of them.* Give them away or pack them in a suitcase where you don't have to look at them every day and wonder when you'll be thin enough to wear them again. Plan a 'clothes' day with your friends: ask everyone to bring clothes they no longer wear, and when they arrive with their bundles, put them in piles on the floor. Look through the piles, let everyone try clothes on. You can all go home with something new to wear.

● **Buy yourself** some new clothes, silky clothes, pretty clothes, clothes that feel good and look good NOW. I realize that you want to wait until you lose weight to buy clothes that you like. Why, you ask, should you spend money on clothes for a body size that you want to change?

Because your ideal body is in the future. And this body, the one you've got right now, is the one you have to walk around with every day. Every time you dress it in clothes that aren't pleasing to you, in fabrics and styles and textures that you don't like, you are punishing yourself.

Squeezing yourself into clothes that are too tight will not help you lose weight. The discomfort will not motivate you; it will not force you into getting thinner. It will, however, cut off your circulation, make it hard to breathe, make it hard to concentrate. It will also give you cause to feel as if you are spilling out of your clothes. Wearing clothes that are too tight makes you feel like a restricted, breathless slob. And wearing clothes that you don't like, in colours or textures that don't please you, is another way of telling yourself that you've been bad and so you have to pay the consequences.

Think of your clothes as costumes. Use them as antidotes to your moods: When you're lethargic, wear something bright and bold. When you're happy, wear something outrageous. Use clothes to counter your feelings; explore the possibilities in muted colours, subtle patterns, soft fabrics, nubby textures.

● **If you can afford it, arrange for a weekly massage with a professional masseuse.** If not, trade weekly massages with a friend. Allow your body – all of it – to be touched by someone who does not have a vested interest in your weight. We often don't claim our bodies; we cut ourselves off at the neck, identifying with our thoughts, our feelings, our faces, while our arms and legs remain strangers. Massage helps to reunite us with our bodies; it provides us with physical pleasure that is not sexual. During a massage no one wants anything from you but your enjoyment at being touched.

Having a massage also helps you realize that your body is finite. If a masseuse works on your feet, then your legs, she has to finish with your legs before she works on your torso. That means your legs do not go on forever. (Did you hear that? Your legs do not go on forever.) They have a beginning and an end. Massage gives you a sense of body boundary, and for people who have distorted and hopelessly large body images, this is extremely helpful.

● **Gather pictures of yourself from your childhood through the present.** Look at your body. Has your image of your body consistently been bigger than your body actually was? Or did well-meaning parents, aunts, teachers tell you you were fat? Were you?

● **From magazines, cut pictures of bodies that reflect your ideal size.** Look at those bodies. Are they truly pleasing? Are they anything at all like your body? Could you ever, in a million years, look like that? When will you stop trying?

● **Spend five minutes every day looking at your body in a full-length mirror.** Notice where the curves are, notice the recesses, notice the lines of your arms, the shape of your hands. Notice, observe, but *do not* *judge.* Every time a judgement arises, replace it with an observation – that is, go from 'My arms are flabby' to 'My arms follow a line beginning at my shoulders; they extend on either side of my torso, etc. . . . '

After you do this for a week, begin making a conscious effort at complimenting yourself. 'My skin is creamy.' 'My hair falls in soft curls around my face.' 'My legs are strong and firm.' Each time you look in the mirror, notice *three* qualities that are lovely about your body. At the beginning you may have to stand there for a long time. But it will get easier. And easier.

Look at yourself as if you liked yourself.

Liking yourself will follow.

Making Friends With Ourselves

If I walked over to a man, held a gun to his head, and demanded he have an erection, could he?

In much the same way, we demand of ourselves that we change.

We begin with who we are now. We begin with all the things about ourselves that we don't like. And the things we do like. We begin with our fat and our selfishness and our tenderness and our beauty. We begin by treating ourselves as if we liked ourselves. Now.

No force. No punishment. No threats.

Gentle beginnings, small steps. Now.

● **Make two lists:**

How I Keep Myself Deprived . . .

Ways to Nourish Myself Other Than Eating . . .

and then do one activity on *each* of those lists every day. Sometimes an action as simple as wearing a belt or tucking your shirt in can be enough to bolster your sense of worthiness for that day. Sometimes the changes are bigger, require more time, more thought, more risk. Sometimes you are waiting to get thin to begin your life. And, like so many fifty- and sixty-year-old women I see in Breaking Free workshops, you can spend your life waiting to begin. You can grow old waiting to begin. And then you can die without having ever lived.

When you've used food as both physical and emotional nourishment for years, it may seem, at first, that 'nothing is as good as food.' That's because you've been turning to it for a long time and it has become the quickest, tastiest, and most available source of nourishment. You're practised at using food; you know how. It's familiar and because it's familiar, it's comfortable. But it is also uncomfortable because when you are not hungry and use food to nourish yourself, whatever it was in you that needed nourishment is still hungry.

People ask me what I do to nourish myself without food, and I tell them that what I do might not nourish them and that they have to find their own ways. Then they say, 'We know that. But what do you do?'

I take jasmine bubble baths. I put candles in the bathroom, even in the afternoon, and I play Georgia Kelly's* harp music. If I'm having a stressful day, I take two baths, sometimes three. If it's a three-bath-a-day day, I go to sleep at 8:00 P.M. and hope that tomorrow will be better.

I cry.

I take walks on the beach.

I buy new pens.

I go to pet stores and look at the puppies.

* To order her music, you can write to Heru Records, P.O. Box 954, Topanga, CA 90290.

I fill my house with flowers, especially irises, every week.

I dance.

I write in my journal.

What kinds of things do you like to do?

If you weren't frightened of indulging yourself, what would you do to indulge yourself?

Taking care of yourself, courting yourself, takes practice. It's not as simple as deciding that you want to care for yourself so you will. You wouldn't expect to pick up a violin for the first time and be able to play like Isaac Stern. Yet you will probably expect to do the right things, even if they're nourishing, immediately. But it doesn't work that way. Living well, nourishing yourself, becoming yourself takes time. But what else is there to do?

● **If your feelings of unworthiness are overwhelming, or if you think you might need concentrated attention, I suggest you work with a psychotherapist.** Individual therapy can be extremely valuable in facilitating growth; a therapist has no vested interest in how you change, whereas friends and family do because their lives are so inextricably bound up with, and affected by, yours.

I began therapy when I quit my preparations for medical school; I was confused and uncertain (and overweight). My therapist's unconditional acceptance of me, her quiet but rock-steady belief in me, her constant encouragement that I discover work I truly loved rather than settle for work that would please my family gave me permission to flourish.

I often encourage participants in Breaking Free workshops to see a therapist while they are attending the workshop. It is helpful to have both group and one-on-one support.

Be discriminating about whom you choose as a therapist. Remember that you are choosing a partner, someone who can participate in and encourage your growth. Ask your friends or teachers for referrals. Make a few initial appointments; if you don't like the first two or three therapists, ask for more referrals. Call the local women's centre or university counselling centre. Don't settle; don't try to please anyone but yourself. The decision is important enough for you to be as discriminating as it takes to find the right person. (Note: There is a difference between right and perfect. There is no perfect therapist, just as there is no perfect person.)

If you want to work on your eating problems, ask the person you choose if she is familiar with eating disorders. If she is not, and you like her very much, bring her *Fat Is A Feminist Issue*, by Susie Orbach; Kim Chernin's *The Obsession*, and my own *Feeding The Hungry Heart*. A good therapist should be able to work with you and your relationship with food even if she is unfamiliar with the specifics. Eating and food are metaphors for living and for growing. Hungering issues are not restricted to over- or under-eating.

If you cannot afford private, individual therapy, seek out a health collective or a women's centre or a family services centre. (In many parts of the country there are reputable therapists for as little as fifteen dollars an hour. If that's too expensive for you on a weekly basis, go every other week. But go.)

● **Begin saying no.** Many of the women who come to me do not set limits. They feel they can't say no, or they wouldn't be loved. They feel that they give and give, do things they don't especially want to do, and then they have to eat to replenish themselves to get something back. They use their weight, not their voices, to say no.

Being able to say no, to establish limits (and to notice

that you're still loved or respected) helps to develop the
sense that you are loved for who you are. When you turn
yourself inside out to be loved, you feel that who you
really are is not good or nice or kind enough. You have to
hide yourself. And so you eat.

I encourage participants in workshops to say no once a
day to something they don't want to do but would ordinarily agree to. But I encourage them to be discriminating about whom they say no to.

Pick a safe person, someone who loves you, someone
who respects your feelings. Practise with them. Does
the world shatter when you refuse a request? Are you
left alone after saying no? Refuse simple requests at
first: going to the grocery store, answering the phone,
doing a favour. Notice what happens in your body when
you say no. Does your heart beat faster? Are you
frightened? What happens after you've said no, after
they have responded? Do you regret saying no? Do you
feel that you've cared for yourself? Are you glad?

● **Write a letter to yourself.** Begin it with 'Dear ——,
I love you because . . . ' and spare yourself no immodesty.

● **Forgive Yourself, Forgive Someone Else.** In
Breaking Free workshops, we do a forgiveness exercise
borrowed from Stephen Levine's book *Who Dies* (Anchor
Books, 1982). First, you visualize someone whom you
resent and you say 'I forgive you.' You spend time
imagining this person, feeling him or her in your heart.
You say 'I forgive you' and you notice what happens:
whether it's difficult, whether or not you're still angry.
Then you visualize someone from whom you wish to *ask*
forgiveness. You picture him in your heart and ask his
forgiveness for all the things you've said and done that
caused him pain: 'For all those words that were said out
of forgetfulness or fear. Out of my closedness, out of my

confusion. I ask your forgiveness.' And last, you visualize yourself. Using your own first name, you say to yourself, 'I forgive you.'

Some people find it hard to forgive someone else; most find it hardest to forgive themselves.

The question of anger arises: Why should we let go of anger? If it's justified, if someone has wronged us, why should we let go?

The question of self-indulgence arises: If we forgive ourselves, if we truly feel that we are all right, what will present us from repeating our actions?

Anger has its place and it has its time. It seems to me that it's extremely valuable if it can be expressed without intentionally hurting the other person or attacking him in a way that causes him to get angry in return. Using 'I' statements ('I am angry because I feel you are not listening to me') instead of 'you' statements ('You never listen to me, you only care about yourself') gives him a chance to hear you evaluate what you're saying, a chance to hear that he's hurt you.

Anger is a way of saying 'I will take so much and I won't take any more. You've crossed the line and now I want you to stop.' Anger is a way to set limits.

Many compulsive eaters eat because they are angry and they don't know they are allowed to say so. But no one else knows what they are eating about. The person to whom the anger is directed has no idea that cookies are unspoken words. Using their anger against themselves, compulsive eaters turn it to fat, which then turns into self-hatred. Years later, when I see them in a workshop, they are still angry at their mothers or their lovers. And they are still eating to express that anger. Even after fifteen years. Even if the person they are angry at is dead.

Anger needs to be recognized and, most of the time, it needs to be expressed. The person does not have to be in front of you; the person does not have to be alive. You can, with the help of a therapist or a support group led by a therapist, release anger by talking to a pillow as if it were the person you want to address.

You can also write a letter. Begin it with, 'I am angry at you because . . . ' and write it all down. You don't have to mail it. This is for you.

A few years ago, I was driving in a car with a friend of mine; I was telling him that I was angry about something he did and he said, 'One moment of anger destroys a hundred years of virtuous deeds.' If I'd been able to remain calm, I'd have said, 'Good. Now I'm going to destroy 10,000 years of virtue because, at this moment, I'd like to kill you.'

The lack of permission to get angry, the idea that we should be big-hearted enough to overlook whatever it is that we're angry about, can escalate the seriousness of an already difficult situation.

Sometimes it's appropriate to express your anger immediately and sometimes it isn't. (It is *always* appropriate to acknowledge your anger to yourself.) Ask yourself what you want, what your purpose is in expressing anger. If, when you get angry, you are verbally abusive, then expressing it immediately does not help you or anyone else. It is helpful, in such a case, to wait until you can say what will truly get across your feelings: how you are hurt, why you are hurt, what you want the other person to know.

For me, it is the communication, the heartfelt exchange, that is crucial. I want to feel I can say what is on my mind, in my heart, that the other person can hear me, that I can hear her and then that we can move on. If

I express a feeling, it is in order to be able to move through it instead of staying stuck and whirling in the heat of it.

Sometimes I can move through anger by myself. Sometimes I can see where I get caught, the erroneous assumptions I make. I can detach myself from the situation and from the heat of my feelings to see the situation objectively. Or at least somewhat objectively.

And sometimes I can't. At those times it takes courage to say 'I am angry.' It takes courage because anger is an admission of vulnerability. It is as much as saying 'What you said, who you are, affects me and matters to me.' If you let someone know that, then who knows what he will do? He might not care. He might hurt you again. He might leave.

The expression of anger is also an admission that you are not perfect, that you are not forgiving enough to let go of this particular incident.

Both of these feelings – vulnerability and imperfection – are disturbing. But that doesn't mean they are wrong or need to be pushed away.

If you have already given words to your anger and are still angry, or if it is an old hurt, you can ask yourself which is more important: being right or deepening the relationship?

Sometimes we are in relationships we wish we were out of. And because we don't have the courage to end them, and because endings are painful and lonely, we stay. And we fight. And the fights become bitter and hateful. When we can't give ourselves permission to leave, we use our fights to prove to ourselves and everyone around us that our partner is mean or hopelessly thoughtless. We *don't want* to forgive; we want to be *right*. The fights become a contest of wills. We are no longer fighting about what we are fighting about; we are fighting for our lives. And we're not about to give up.

If you find yourself in a situation like this, the issue of forgiveness is secondary to the terror of endings and being alone. It is important to distinguish between the difficulty of forgiving – compromising, letting go on your side, giving up being right – and not wanting to forgive. If you discover that you don't want to forgive, then the reasons for that – your terror of being alone or your self-worth or your right to choose a person whom you truly want to be with – are what need your attention. You have to feel that you are giving yourself a gift by letting go of anger, that you are expanding yourself, not diminishing yourself. Relationships, friendships as well as partnerships, are hard work. You must want to be there, you must want to stay there, you must want to send down your roots and grow there.

Forgiving yourself is another matter.

What if it turns out that we're deep-down bad?

What if we keep repeating the same mistakes?

What if we alienate everyone we love because we are so lenient with ourselves that they see the truth of us: our thoughtlessness, our selfishness, our meanness?

Forgiving yourself is not only an expression of your vulnerability and imperfection, but is also a leap of faith in your intentions. You are no more bad or good than anyone else. The difference between someone who kills and someone who doesn't is that the first person acts on what the second person only thinks about.

We are all capable of the most awful atrocities. The difference between those who commit them and those who don't is that the latter are willing to acknowledge their impulses, their darkness, to forgive themselves for it and to move toward the light. They work with, rather than act upon, their impulses by admitting them, not by denying or repressing them.

When you forgive yourself, you express an intention to work with the darkness within you. You admit that you are not perfect, that you've hurt people you love, that you probably will do so again. Forgiving yourself expresses a willingness to *learn* from your fragility and your fallibility instead of pretending they are not there.

Being Forgiving About Not Being Forgiving

WITH YOURSELF

● **Write down all the things about yourself – everything you've done or said or thought – that are unforgivable.** Be very specific; be all-inclusive.

Now take a look. How bad *are* those things? I know you think they're bad, but really – how bad?

● **Say 'I forgive you' to yourself after each one of the items you've written down above.**

Notice what happens.

What benefits are you receiving from not forgiving yourself? What are you trying to prove?

Are you frightened you would go wild?

Is that a reality?

Do you want to go wild?

● **Write a portrait of yourself as a person who could be forgiven.** What would you have to do, say, be, wear to forgive yourself?

Does this person you describe, this forgivable you, make mistakes?

● **Imagine that you are forgiven.**
What do you do now?
What do you think about? How does your life change?

WITH SOMEONE ELSE

● **'Ask' yourself if you want to forgive.**
I suspect you already know the answer. You don't
have to act on it, but at least be honest with yourself.

● **If you don't want to forgive,** *that's all right.*
Maybe you have not fully expressed yourself.
Maybe you are not satisfied with the outcome of the
argument.
Maybe you don't want to be in the relationship.
Whatever you feel, you cannot begin dealing with it,
even if you want to, until you know what it is.
Your choices are not about *what* you feel; they are
about what you do with what you feel.
So – how do you feel?

● **If you want to forgive but are having difficulty,**
remind yourself that it's hard to let go of being
right. Forgive yourself for being unforgiving.
Look inside yourself. Is there anger there that hasn't
been expressed? What would you lose, what would you
be giving up, if you forgave?

● **It helps to cry.** It helps to talk to pillows. It helps to
smash pillows. When your anger is deep and old, make
sure you are not alone when you begin expressing it. If
you are not in therapy, ask a friend, someone you trust,
to be with you. When you know that someone is with
you, you can let yourself go and not be afraid that you'll
drown in your feelings.

● **If you have expressed your anger and are still angry, set some time aside each day to do the forgiveness exercise described on page 212.** And then, as you go through the days, imagine yourself forgiving the person who is the object of your anger. What happens? What do you have to give up to forgive them? What would forgiving say about yourself? Maybe you are angry at yourself for staying in the relationship too long, maybe you are angry at yourself for something else, and this other-directed anger is a way of deflecting your self-directed anger. If this is true, if the anger you feel is toward yourself, you can work on that, too. (You can forgive yourself, remember?)

Many of us are afraid that if we allow ourselves to feel our anger, it will never end. Feelings that are pushed away get stronger. It's no wonder we're frightened of them, but they *do* end. No feeling, once expressed, has ever lasted a lifetime. Or even six months. If you let it begin, it will end.

On Powerful Women

Part of being powerful is learning to say no. But it goes beyond that.

Being powerful is giving yourself permission to feel good. Being powerful is allowing yourself to be as creative, outrageous, honest, sensual, and demanding as you are. Being powerful is realizing that you don't have to hide anything from anyone.

Most of the women I work with are afraid that if they lost weight, they would be *too* powerful. One woman said, 'I would scare everyone away. I would mow them down.' They are frightened that losing weight would make them perfect, since being fat, in their eyes, is their single most tragic flaw. And they are afraid that being perfect would threaten everyone around them.

I agree. I would feel very threatened by a perfect human being. But I'm not worried; I've never met one.

Many of us keep ourselves focused on food and disliking our bodies because we are afraid of what would happen if we didn't. We're afraid of being called bitchy and arrogant and aggressive and demanding. We're afraid of becoming ball-breaking amazons.

Those are fears. Those are myths. We need to reckon with them. Now.

Although it is true, and I have heard it from many men, that there is something threatening about a woman who is successful and expressive and attractive, it is also true that since the women's movement began in the sixties, many more successful, expressive women are becoming visible. We are no longer anomalies. There *is* support for women who refuse to deny their capabilities; there are women's network organizations, women's centres, women's banks, women's business organizations. And there are men who are willing to be emotionally supportive of strong women while facing their fears about them. We are living in a time of tremendous change. We are trail blazers.

BUT

Being successful, expressive, powerful *does not mean* being perfect.

Too many women associate being thin with always being in control. They associate being thin with being the centre of attention, with being successful, with always having to get it right. Nothing is ever an 'always.' Imagining *that* is the fastest way to make it a 'never.' You will *never* allow yourself to be powerful if it means that when you are, you are not allowed to cry.

Our images, not the reality, of women without weight problems keep us stuck. We're afraid of our potential for power. We're afraid that other people will become afraid, and we're afraid that there won't be any room for our fragility. The former fear, while grounded in reality, is changing as a result of the cultural prevalence of visibly successful women. The latter fear is an internal image that needs to be named, brought to daylight, and worked with.

Ask yourself – now – what would happen if you were to become as powerful as you are?

Who would be frightened?

How would your life change?

How would you eat?

What would you wear?

What kinds of things would upset you?

How would you walk, talk?

What kind of work would you do?

Who would be your friends?

Does your life, the way it is now, support you in becoming powerful?

Do one powerful thing today.

Tomorrow, when you wake up, dress as you would if you were expressing your power. Then walk through the day as a powerful woman would.

Treat yourself as if you were *already enough*.

Courting ourselves or another person is a time of delight and discovery.

Sometimes it lasts six months, sometimes it lasts a year.

Courting is important; it establishes a foundation of delight and laughter upon which we can later draw.

And draw we will. Because after courting comes friendship. And friendship, with ourselves or with another, is hard work.

When, at fifteen, I moved to a different city and became the new girl in school, Denise Marks approached me and said, 'Don't worry about making friends, you'll have lots of them. You have long straight hair and the people around here like that.'

Those of us who rip ourselves apart because we don't have thin enough bodies say the same sort of thing. We say that friendship, liking ourselves, depends on how we look. And that when we are overweight we are failures and undeserving of our own respect, much less of anyone else's.

Friendship, real friendship, has nothing to do with anything as physical as long straight hair. Or body weight. It requires commitment and perseverance. It requires a willingness to stay and thrash it out when staying and thrashing it out is the last thing you want to do.

'I'm a leaver,' someone in a Breaking Free workshop said last week. 'When the going gets rough, I bail out.' She may leave relationships but, more important, she leaves herself.

Friendship takes practice. We need to *learn* how to stay and thrash it out; it is not a skill that we are born with.

Friendship requires compassion. We're *not* perfect; we *will* make mistakes; we *will* overeat. But we're doing our best and that's good enough.

14
On Pain:
'Life is Hard.
Then You Die.'*

'Good people don't feel pain.'

A Breaking Free workshop participant

Everyone is in pain about something.

There isn't any place to put pain.

There isn't anything to do with it.

In a world in which you witness death of people you love or they witness yours, there is no way out.

I'm not sure when I stopped waiting for the end of the fairy tale to begin. Maybe it was the day I found out that *Feeding the Hungry Heart* (originally called *Is There Life After Chocolate?*) was going to be bought for publication . . .

It was a wonderful day. When I walked into Bobbs-Merrill, the receptionist, two secretaries, and my editor were wearing shiny blue buttons that said, 'Things are getting worse . . . please send chocolate.' I was taken to lunch and told that the manuscript was going to become a book. I shrieked, the editor laughed and a fortune-teller came to our table and told me I would be very successful. Later in the day, I met my father at the Algonquin Hotel and he said, 'Many famous writers gathered here before you.' When I arrived at my mother's house that night, we sat on her bed, opened a bottle of champagne, and toasted the success of the book. After my mother and stepfather went to sleep,

* Seen emblazoned on a T-shirt in Santa Cruz, California.

I sat in the den and wrote in my journal. A fire was crackling in the fireplace, the clock on the wall chimed twice. Suddenly I began to cry.

I'd dreamed about being a writer since fifth grade when I had written a story about a girl who fills in for an airline stewardess and saves the plane from disaster when everyone, including the pilot, gets food poisoning. I wrote constantly – stories, poems, letters. I wrote because I had to write, because writing made sense of shards and fragments of experience. I wrote because I couldn't imagine *not* writing. And all the while I dreamed secretly that someday someone would discover my work.

Then someone did. Twenty years of anticipation for this moment, in the den with the clock and the fire and the sounds of night. I was ecstatic; I was also alone. No one to glow to, no one to tell. I felt like the collar of a shirt without the cardboard. No other dreams to hold me up.

The pain was still there. Lodged between my bones, the pain that has no particular cause was still there. That rumpled, formless emptiness. I cried in the den and then I cried myself to sleep. I cried because I knew, perhaps for the first time, that if the realization of a childhood dream didn't take the pain away, nothing ever would. And I cried because I knew then that I was going to be in some kind of pain, always, for the rest of my life.

The pain of childbirth. The pain of illness. The pain of disappointment. The pain of waiting. The pain of separation. The pain of never feeling good enough. The pain of being too young. The pain of arguments. The pain of rejection. The pain of risking. The pain of failing. The pain of headaches, broken bones. The pain of forgetting, the pain of remembering. The pain of getting old.

The pain of never knowing when you or anyone you love will die. The pain of death, and the everyday pain of being alive, of loneliness and grief and sadness and fear. The pain of knowing that the world could end in a nuclear holocaust – today, tomorrow, next year.

If we could separate moments, if we could separate the ones we don't like, the ones that cause us discomfort, from the ones we do like, the piles, if we were lucky, would be equal. We spend *at least* half our lives in either physical or emotional discomfort, yet we persist in believing that happiness is our natural, normal condition and that when we're not happy, we're not normal.*

When I ask the women in a workshop about pain, they say:

> 'Good people don't feel pain. If I did things right, I wouldn't be in pain.'
> 'Being in pain means I'm being punished.'
> 'It's because I've been a bad mother.'
> 'If I let myself feel even a little pain, the other pains that I've pushed away will come back. I can't. It's too much.'
> 'I'm afraid that pain will eat me up, so I eat it first.'

We think we're supposed to be happy and when we're not, we think we're being punished. Then we try to figure out why we're being punished. We wonder what is so terribly wrong with us. We wonder if we are bad people. That thought is itself so painful that we push it away, and when the pain continues, we think we're being punished.

Whoever told us that we're supposed to be happy was wrong.

I think that 'happily ever after' should be struck from

* I am indebted to Sharon Salzburg for this idea.

every story in which it appears unless there is an addendum that reads, 'This is just a fairy tale. Real people don't live happily ever after.'

Real people feel some kind of discomfort every day of their lives. Being born hurts. Living hurts. Dying hurts. If we know that, if we don't expect to be happy all the time, then we don't have to feel frightened or cursed when, inevitably, we are in pain. The expectation that pain is bad, abnormal, or avoidable creates fear and confusion when pain arises. It also creates varied and complex systems within us that are designed to avoid pain at all costs.

Most people never touch the bottom of their pain. They become compulsive instead, and in so doing, they exchange one pain, that of being alive, for another, the pain of compulsion.

Neither road is easy. Compulsion is painful and living without compulsion is painful. Compulsion has its joys; so does living without it. The biggest advantage I see in living without compulsion is that you stop being afraid of pain.

In Breaking Free workshops, we do an exercise that involves sitting, just sitting, when pain arises. Because our immediate impulse is to run from pain, sitting with it necessitates being aware of the moment before you run. Feeling pain and avoiding it are so entwined that it is often difficult to separate the two; it takes practice.

When people sit instead of eat, they discover that pain is cyclical, not linear. Pain washes over them, then it recedes. Pain moves. Pain changes. Pain ends.

Pain ends.

Pain comes and goes and then it's over. Even chronic pain comes in cycles. Even sharp, first-time pain changes from moment to moment. What we call pain is sensation: burning, vibrating, tingling, aching, pulsing, throbbing, sinking. If you examine the throb of a headache or heartache, if you soften instead of tighten around pain, it will change as you watch. It will move from pulsing to tingling, from gnarly to smooth. It may go from being round and bright red to being flat and deep orange. It will change texture and location and shape and consistency. Pain comes with the territory of being alive. Suffering is extra. Suffering is what happens when we react to pain by pushing it away.

Most of what we call pain is suffering. Most pain is our reaction to the fear of what would happen if we let ourselves feel the pain. Most pain is resistance to pain. Resistance to pain makes us wild, desperate, frenzied – and increases the pain. We'll do anything to knock it out. If the pain is physical, we'll take anything; if the pain is emotional, we'll eat anything. Anything, anything to make it go away.

But something happens in the process of trying not to feel what we can't help but feel: we contract, become smaller and smaller, take up residence in the upper left corner of our chest. We stop taking risks, we close ourselves off, we steel ourselves for living. We curl around ourselves like sea anemones, like morning glories in the evening. We get addicted to the means by which we avoid pain. And then we feel isolated and crazy because we are living in a haze of numbness and are missing our lives.

It's not a matter of changing what you eat. It's a matter of changing how you live. When you work on the root level of compulsion, and begin allowing yourself to experience discomfort, then you won't need to eat to push it away.

I know that's asking a lot. No one likes pain; no one would choose pain. But it's here whether we choose it or not. I'm not asking you to reach out your arms, to invite and seek pain as you would a lover. What I do ask is that you learn to investigate and examine pain, and that you begin to accept it for what it is: a natural consequence of being alive.

What Shape Is Your Pain?

● **Spend five minutes apiece on the following lists:**

1. Begin with *Pain Is* . . . and then quickly allow yourself, without considering your responses, to complete the list. If the answers are simple, childlike, or monosyllabic, fine. 'Pain is bad' or 'Pain is awful.' Allow the conditioned responses, the associations, and feelings about pain to surface.

2. Next, complete the sentence: *When I Am In Pain* . . . Again, allow immediate and unconsidered responses to surface. Are you afraid of pain because it makes you vulnerable? Are you afraid because you worry that it will never end? Because you don't know how to ask for help?

After you've completed the lists, read them over and notice their tone. Is your predominant reaction to pain one of avoidance or acceptance? What do you learn about your expectations of pain from the lists? Is it apparent that you think you should be happy most of the time? That you feel as though pain is a punishment?

These lists, like the others in the book, are tools for observation. They give you insight into the unconscious assumptions and beliefs on which many of your actions are based. They let you know where you are starting from.

● **Think back on the messages you received as a child when you were in pain.**

What happened when you cried?

Were you sent to your room?

Were you told to stop?

Were you punished, comforted, bribed?

How have those messages affected your willingness to experience pain?

When I cried, I'd frighten myself because I frightened the people around me. My father used to hold me and whisper, 'Stop now. That's enough. Stop crying.' I used to gulp back my tears, hiccup on them for a few minutes, and then walk around wet-eyed and weepy for an hour or so.

My friend Ellen says that 'At a certain point when I cried, my mother would say, "Okay. That's it," and I had to come out of my room and join the rest of the family.'

'Hold yourself in'; 'Get yourself under control'; 'Crying is a sign of weakness'; 'Only babies cry.'

Who says? Why not? What's wrong with crying?

When I feel tears welling up in my throat, I let them (provided I am in a place where I can cry). If it's the middle of the day, I put my head down on my desk and cry. Sometimes, I feel like a child again, waiting for someone to find me, to put their arms around me and tell me to 'Shush, now, that's enough.' I think that because I'm crying, it means that something is wrong and I'd better not let myself down into it because there's no one around to pull me out.

Something *is* wrong, and I'm crying about whatever it is. It took me a long time and many hiccuped tears to understand that it's all right; when I let myself cry, the sadness washes through me and sooner or later, I feel better, pick myself up, and go on through the day.

The last time I was in New York, my father came to

visit on a day that I was feeling lonely. When he asked how I felt, I started to cry. He put his arms around me and said, 'Okay now . . . shh. There's no need for tears.'

And I said, 'There is, too. Crying is good for me – for you too, Dad, if you'd ever let yourself. And I'm going to keep on crying until the tears stop.' He laughed. So did I. And that was that.

● **Allow yourself a half hour each day to be miserable.**

Pick a time, either in the early morning or evening, when you won't be disturbed. Or pick what is generally your most miserable time of the day. If you choose the same time each day, and call it your miserable time, you can incorporate the routine as an ordinary and acceptable part of what you do.

Begin the half hour by thinking about all the things you are unhappy about. Keep naming them until you can't think of any more. Then, as they say, go for it. Do something about all this misery. Act it out in a particular way: cry, lie down on the floor, mope around the house, write a bittersweet poem or a poison pen letter, make a picture of a skull and crossbones.

When the half hour is up, go on with your day.

● **Draw your pain.** Get some crayons and plain white drawing paper. Now, allow an image of either a specific pain in your life or a kind of general because-you're-alive pain to present itself. Is it an animal? A man? A mythical creature? Is it large? Is it dark? Put it on paper. Externalize it. See that it can have a beginning and an end.

● **The next time you're in physical pain, sit down wherever you can.** Close your eyes and take five minutes to answer the following questions:

Where in your body is the pain?

What colour is the pain?

What shape?

Does it move or is it stationary?

Does it have a texture?

When we're in pain, we often conjure up images of what would happen if the pain didn't go away. A few months ago, I awoke with a stiff neck and a headache. When, after two days, it had gotten worse, I remembered a book I once read about a child who was taken to the doctor because of a chronic stiff neck and diagnosed as having a brain tumour. Within a week, I convinced myself that I too had a brain tumour and would be dead in six months. I began planning the wrenching bedside scenario: my mother, my father, my brother, Sara. I started feeling very sorry for myself because I was going to die without having met Mr Right Enough and before my second book would be published. Every time I moved my head, the stiffness in my neck reminded me that I was dying. And it was because of that image, as well as because of the actual sensations, that I winced and tightened when I felt pain.

If I gently brought myself back to the actual sensations of pain, to the present moment instead of images that being in pain evoked, I relaxed. When I stopped resisting the pain, it changed. It softened.

With practice, anyone can learn the difference between a stiff neck and a brain tumour.

● **Sit in a comfortable chair and think back to a recent time when you ate compulsively.** With your eyes closed, recount the incident, the triggering emotion that set you reeling to food . . . See yourself eating exactly as you did . . . Notice how you ate, what you ate, if you tasted the food. How you felt about yourself when you were through . . . Now, as if you were flipping the pages of a book, recount again the triggering incident. This time, in your fantasy, create a place for yourself to sit down before you eat. When you're seated, focus on the feelings in your body. Give them a name. Are you sad? Angry? Lonely? Hurt? Frightened? Where is that particular emotion? Does it have a colour? A shape? What happens as you sit there watching . . . Does the emotion change location in your body? Does it change intensity? Sit there for a few minutes and watch the emotion and its corresponding sensations as they change. Now, in your fantasy, get up and do the next thing you did that day. Do you still want to eat? Are your feelings about yourself different from what they were when you ate?

This exercise, done repeatedly, can help you enter into the pain that you usually eat to avoid. A major reason we eat is that we're afraid that the pain is bigger than we are, that 'It will eat me before I can eat it.' When you've gone through this exercise two or three times, you'll see that although a situation may be incredibly painful, may hurt more than any hurt you've experienced, it won't destroy you. You feel pain, you hurt from pain, and then you get up and go on with your life. The pain doesn't necessarily go away but it does change, it does recede into the background for a while. If it's a big pain, it returns. And then you feel it again. And it recedes again.

If you know that pain – any pain, no matter how huge, even the pain that comes from the death of someone you love – will not last forever or rip you apart, then you can allow yourself to experience it fully. When you allow the depth of pain to take its natural course, it comes to its natural end. When you push away an emotion, it remains in the wings of your heart, waiting to enter, threatening you, haunting you with shadows.

● **The next time someone you love is in pain, don't try to make it go away.** Don't kiss it and make it better. Be with that person without trying to make him happy. Notice the tendency to comfort him, to tell him it's going to be all right. Notice how difficult it is to see someone in pain – it brings up your own – and see him anyway. Stay with him, quietly. You don't have to say anything. Just being there, allowing him the presence and the love of another human being while he experiences what is truly and only his – the pain – is a gift that few are capable of giving.

One of the sweetest times I've spent with another person was a morning when I was very sad and didn't want to talk about why. A friend was with me and, sensing that words were unnecessary, he sat next to me for a long, long time in silence.

I felt as if he were a clear, still lake in the heat of summer. I dived into him, kicked my legs, made circles, ripples, then surfaced. I felt free to move, sensing that he would be there waiting when I stopped. After the tears, he held me, kissed my eyes. Then we talked about something else.

Be like a lake, a still summer lake where lilies grow.

15

On Sexuality:*
'Men Use Sex the Way
Women Use Food.'**

'I feel like men see me as boobs with a woman attached.'

A Breaking Free workshop participant

I was kissed for the first time in eighth grade. I don't mean one of those spin-the-bottle kisses or an in-the-closet-for-three-seconds kiss. This kiss was real.

Larry Klein was a tenth-grader and, as such, was an older man. He put his arms around me, pressed his lips to mine, stuck his tongue in my mouth, and held me tight. My eyes rolled in my head. This was kissing? Someone's tongue in my mouth? If this was what movie stars did, it was disgusting. I pushed Larry away. He persisted. 'Part of the reason you don't like it,' he said, 'is because your eyes are open. You can't *stare* when you kiss; you have to close your eyes, get in the right mood.' I agreed to try it again, this time with my eyes closed.

During the next year and a half, Larry assumed the role of sexual mentor. His were the first hands I felt under my Danskin shirts. His were the first hands I removed from my Danskin shirts. His were the first fingers that crept under my skirts. And his were the first fingers I removed from my skirts. Until one day when I didn't remove them any longer.

* I'd like to thank Debby Burgard for her generosity with her time and ideas on this subject.

** From the mouth of a Breaking Free workshop participant. Thank you.

With Larry, I learned that my body, quite apart from my real self, was an object of fascination to boys. With Larry, I learned that I could use my body as bait to lure them and as a weapon to punish them. With Larry, I learned that it was easier to say yes and let them touch me than to say no and fight with them. With Larry, I learned to go numb.

The scene shifts. I am sixteen and dating Sheldon Heller with the coal black eyes and skin like an American Indian's. On our fourth date, he kisses me lightly. After a few months, he has made no move to feel my breasts, touch my body. I wonder what is wrong and ask him. He says, 'I only do that with girls I don't like. With you, it's special.' When I visit him during the summer at Brown's Hotel in the Pocono Mountains, I see a score card that he and his friends are keeping: Whoever sleeps with the most girls wins. After eight months, he still has not touched my body.

Now I am twenty-two and living with Jason. The beginning of our relationship is fiery and passionate. We make love in the afternoon, in the middle of the night. Anytime. Anywhere. Within two years, I do not want to make love as much as he. When I wake up in the morning and I feel his hard penis against my back, I turn away, make excuses. When we finally do make love, I think of other things: the laundry, my work. I want it to be over. He feels rejected; I feel guilty. We both assume I am frigid.

At twenty-eight, I gain fifty-five pounds and my sexual perspective takes an abrupt about face. I am the fattest I have ever been and I feel ugly and withdrawn. But I also feel something that stuns me: I feel relieved. I'm

tired of the burden of a woman's body. I'm tired of the
looks from the men who unload the luggage at the air-
port. I'm tired of the bind I feel: resenting men for wanting me sexually but using my sexuality to pull them in.
I'm tired but I'm frightened; I don't know what else I
have of value besides my body.

During the next two years, I work hard at discovering
my unspoken beliefs about my body and my sexuality
and how related these beliefs are to my feelings and
fears about work and intimacy. In therapy, Alexandra
and I spend many sessions talking about my fear of saying no, my need to be loved at the cost of my integrity. I
keep daily records of my food intake and my feelings
before and after I eat.

I realize that when I am thin, I feel out of control. I feel
like I *have* to be enchanting, energetic, and seductive. I
have to use what I've got – my body – to get what I want:
attention, love, closeness.

The real problem is not whether or not I am thin but
that I feel such inner poverty. I am frightened that who
I am is hard and selfish and that unless I mask myself in
a beautiful body, the essential me will be discovered.

Although being fat hides me in layers of flesh, it
paradoxically reveals me for who I am: When I am fat, I
do not have to pretend that I am not afraid. I do not have
to pretend that I am interested when I am bored or that
I am feeling seductive when I want to be alone. I do not
have to pretend anything at all. Being fat gives me permission to listen to myself because I assume that no one
else is interested. By taking the crutch of culturally
defined attractiveness away, being fat forces me to
stand on my own for the first time in my life.

Like any beginner, I take small steps: I practise saying no. I practise asking, expressing my vulnerability. I

join a writing workshop, send a story to a woman who is editing an anthology.

Soon, when I look in the mirror, I notice the curves of my body, the hollows and recesses of my arms, legs, breasts. I learn to appreciate my body for my own pleasure. I spend a year alone and without any lovers.

Now, years later, I still from time to time doubt myself, am critical of my body, wonder if I am worth loving. But I don't pretend anymore. And often for weeks at a stretch, I feel like treasure that's been discovered after three hundred years of lying on the ocean floor.

Food and sex.

Most women that seek help in Breaking Free workshops feel that being thin necessitates being flirtatious, bubbly, and sexual, *all the time*. Being thin means walking down the street and getting wolf-whistled, hey-honeyed, and undressed with stares. Being thin means being approached by undesirable men at parties, on buses, at work, anywhere. It means never knowing whether you are valued for your body or your intelligence, vision, and sensitivity. Being thin means increasing the possibility of being raped.

The women who come to Breaking Free workshops torture themselves because they are not thin and then sabotage themselves by eating compulsively. They consciously define being thin as their ultimate personal goal while unconsciously avoiding it as their ultimate sexual nightmare.

Some of the women I see have been sexually abused, some have been raped, some have been abandoned by a father or a lover. Some are frightened of intimacy. Most are confused by what it means to be living in an adult woman's body with an adult woman's sexuality, and they use what is forever in the spotlight – their bodies – to express their confusion. They use their bodies as their battlegrounds; they know that in our culture, women's voices may not always be heard, but their bodies will still (and always) be noticed.

Food and sex.

A woman in a Breaking Free workshop says, 'Men use sex the way women use food.' As women, we reach for kisses made of chocolate before kisses on the lips. As women, we find it more acceptable to be fat than to be sexual.

When I was sixteen, a rumour circulated in high school that Lee Van Allen 'went all the way.' Those of us who were still virgins whispered and congregated around the idea like a swarm of bees to jasmine. Lee was the 'bad girl'; she let a boy up into her. She did what all of us dreamed about but would never dare allow.

My mother once told me that if I let Larry's penis anywhere near my vagina, I would get pregnant.

Liddie's mother told her that if she let a boy touch her, he would have no reason to come back. 'He'll use you like a dirty dish rag,' she told her, 'then he'll throw you away.'

Stacey's mother told her, 'All those boys want is sex and if you give it to them, they'll marry someone who won't and come to you for humping.'

We wanted love. We wanted to meet Dr Kildare on the street, dazzle him with our beauty, and live with him forever in a blue clapboard house with red roses growing on the white picket fence. We wanted love and we were taught that you had to choose: If you were a good girl, if you took their hands away from your breasts, you would eventually be rewarded with love and marriage. If you were a bad girl and let them feel you up and finger you,

you'd grow old in fishnet stockings and gold lame mini-skirts – alone. We wanted love and we weren't about to ruin our chances by giving away our biggest advantage, our bargaining power, our bodies.

The messages we received about sex were that it was dirty and that it was a nuisance. Sex was something boys wanted and later, when we got older, that girls tolerated. From the age of twelve until I was twenty-two, I never considered that sex was something that could bring *me* pleasure. I was too busy eating.

During the very same years of puberty and budding breasts, of carrying a black nylon purse to school every day with two sanitary pads, a belt, and an extra pair of underpants, I began obsessing about my thighs. My sexuality, apparent in fantasies of Robert Alsworth's bare chest, was available to me then, was warm and on the surface. I was eleven and wearing my first bra, prancing around the house with my chest stuck out. Fascinated by breasts, I stole a look at my mother's whenever I could. I was impatient for pubic hair and wondered if it would grow in red like Carole Lupell's. The excitement didn't last. Our family doctor, who watched my developing breasts blasted me for gaining weight. My father teased me about getting fat. My mother warned me against getting pregnant. No one celebrated the changes; they feared them instead, and twisted their fears into concerns about my weight. I, in turn, learned to mistrust my ripening body and my hunger for womanly changes. Within a year, my fantasies changed from Robert's almond skin to the lingering taste of a Fig Newton in my mouth.

A woman in a Breaking Free workshop says, 'I was twelve when my body started changing and just about that time, my father started withdrawing. We used to go for rides together on Sunday afternoons, he used to hug and kiss me and hold my hand and then suddenly he grew hostile. He told me to cover myself; he yelled at me because my dresses were too short; he was mean to the boys who came to the house. I started eating a lot. I guess I figured that if I gained enough weight, I could hide my curves and my breasts and my father would take me for rides again.'

Another woman says, 'I developed early; the boys started coming on to me, making fun of me in school. I didn't know what to do. I wanted to be like all the other girls. I gained twenty pounds.'

And another: 'When my breasts got big, I was thirteen. Every year, our family went on a Fourth of July picnic with the next-door neighbours. They had a son who was five years older than me and he'd corner me when we were alone. He'd put his hands in my pants, ask me to kiss his penis. I hated it.'

Before we could be initiated into the wonders of womanhood, we were already sorry. We learned fast that breasts and hips got you in trouble. They got you yelled at, made fun of, pushed away, abused. Better to eat and gain weight than not eat and have the people you love push you away. Or worse, have your uncle/stepfather/older brother/father touch you in funny ways.

Better to erase any signs of womanhood. Better to be fat than to be sexual.

Living in a woman's body is not easy.

Especially if you happen to look like a woman and not like an adolescent boy.

We've spent years trying to slice away what makes our bodies womanly: the roundness, the lushness, and we've sliced our spirits instead. We've listened for so long to what they — our parents, our doctors, our lovers, our fashion moguls, our Hollywood directors — decide is attractive that we've lost our own voices. We don't know who we are anymore.

And we can't wait any longer for them to tell us. We can't wait until they decide that it's acceptable for a woman to look like a woman. We can't wait until they give us permission to enjoy our bodies, until they tell us it's possible that some women are meant to be larger than others. They might always be afraid of bodies that bleed, create, and sustain life. They might always be afraid of women who are unafraid. We can't wait until all the people who fear passionate, powerful women get in touch with those fears instead of projecting them and turning women into sex objects. Their work is to own their fears; our work is to own our power.

Power is born when we stop trying to unzip ourselves out of our bodies, when we stop trying to lose so much weight we look like boys, or gain so much weight we can't be seen. Power is born with the willingness to be seen.

Women are mistrustful of their sexuality because they're mistrustful of their bodies. Until we learn to enjoy our bodies, we cannot possibly enjoy bodily sensations. Until we like our bodies enough to feel worthy of pleasure, we won't be able to recognize it when it comes.

Compulsive eaters are givers. We know how to nurture other people. We're expert at feeding, listening, helping. Convinced that our capacity for pleasure, our appetites for touch and taste and feeling, for wild exuberance would be unmanageable and out of control, we mask our needs by denying their existence, by filling our time with doing for others. For sex to be satisfying, we must be able to receive, not just give, pleasure. And receiving pleasure requires that we allow ourselves to hunger, to be vulnerable enough to ask, need, want.

As girls we learned that sex was dirty and that sex

was a nuisance. We learned that if we let ourselves be sexual, men would use us and throw us away. So we learned to mistrust our bodies and to hide them in too much, or too little, flesh. We learned to deny our hunger and to please others instead of ourselves.

If we learned it, we can unlearn it.

As women, we have choices that we didn't have as girls. We don't have to wear our 'no's' on our bodies. We can say no; we can fight back. We can discriminate between men who see us as 'boobs with a women attached' and men who are respectful of and vulnerable to their own femininity and, therefore, to ours. We can choose our lovers and our friends carefully.

As women, we can learn to be physical and provocative and exuberant for someone we paid little attention to when we were girls. Ourselves.

Most of the women in Breaking Free workshops believe that they can't, they just can't, allow themselves to delight in anything. Their fundamental sense of unworthiness precludes the experience of pleasure from their lives. Even the magnificence of a sunset is discounted by feelings of ugliness. ('If I were thin, then I could really appreciate the colours because then I wouldn't have anything to worry about.') They use their weight as a barrier to delight, forcing it over an obstacle course so laden with self-recrimination that it's dead by the time it gets to their hearts.

Appreciating Your Body

If you are unaccustomed to allowing yourself pleasure, it might be less frightening if you go very slowly in the beginning. The message that you want to give yourself is that 'I'm allowed to feel good. I'm allowed to give myself experiences that enhance my pleasure.'

● **After a bath or a shower, rub oil or lotion into your skin.** Spend an extra few seconds touching the areas of your body that you wish weren't there; they need your loving attention the most. Rub deeply, gently.

● **Browse through an old master drawing book.** Look, really look at the women they drew. Were they skinny and pinched? Were they round and voluptuous? Look through a book of Ruben's or Renoir's painting, Matisse's sculpture. Do their women have flat stomachs and no hips? Are you attracted to these women? Do you find them sensual, lovely, ripe?

● **What exactly do you find attractive?** Find a magazine picture of a very thin model, preferably one in which she is as bare as possible. Look at her bones. Would you want to rub up against them? Look at the angles in her face. Do they please you? Look at her hips. Is there anything about them that suggests she is a woman? Would you find being with her comforting or would you find it intimidating?

Why do you want to be thin? For whom?

● **Be sensual for yourself.** Spend one evening alone in the next week and set up an environment for yourself that you find sensually pleasing. Surround yourself with colours and textures and sounds that make you feel good. Give yourself plenty of time to go from one sensation to another: from a warm bath to a soft nightgown to clean sheets. Go slowly, purposefully. What textures appeal to you? What colours? Notice if you feel guilty about taking so much time for yourself. Notice whose voice you hear telling you that what you are doing is silly or wasteful or wrong.

● **Take a dance class,** a class in which you won't feel

intimidated or judged because of the shape of your body. Try aerobic dancing or jazz dancing.

Dancing is a way to learn how to enjoy your sexuality for yourself; even aerobic dancing can be wild and exuberant. Feel yourself moving, sweating, breathing hard, pushing yourself beyond physical limits, breathing, working, sweating until nothing exists but you and your body.

● **Masturbating** helps you release and enjoy your sexual energy without trying to please someone else. Turn your fantasies loose on the image of your ideal lover. What does he or she look like? Is the body large or small? How does he* walk? Talk? Eat? Does he approach you or do you approach him? Does he communicate with his eyes and hands as well as his lips? How does he touch you? Where does he touch you? Does he talk while he touches you?

Use some elements of your fantasy as ideas with which to experiment; keep them for yourself as reminders of possibilities (but keep in mind that they were born from fantasy).

● **Go to a sauna with women friends.** Notice that no one who lives in her body, who uses her body, looks like a magazine model. Everyone's got saggy breasts or wide hips or cellulite or stretch marks. Or all of them. But they've got their own brands of beauty.

---

* Deciding which pronoun to use has been a delicate issue for me throughout the book. It is awkward to continually use 'he/she' and grammatically incorrect to use 'they.' In many sections, I've used the one that seemed most applicable to the content of the paragraph; in this section, I've used 'he' for convenience, and I apologize if its use in this or any other exercise excludes the participation of gay women.

Learning to Say No

● **Take a women's self-defence class.** Learn how to physically use the power in your body.

● **When someone begins to disturb you, either by calling you names or touching you inappropriately, you have every right to stop them.** If telling them isn't enough, you have to decide what the next appropriate action should be: pushing, screaming, getting someone else's attention, running away.

● **Yes/No.** Try this exercise with a friend: Face each other and decide who will say yes and who will say no. One person looks the other straight in the eye and says 'Yes.' The other does the same but says 'No.' Watch your reactions when you say no. What happens in your body? Do you get afraid? Do you believe yourself? Do you want to say 'I didn't really mean that?'

When you say yes, do you plead or do you say it vehemently? Do you find it easier, more comfortable, more familiar than saying no?

Remember that, just as giving yourself permission to eat gives you permission not to eat, saying no enables you to say yes.

Being Sexual with a Partner

● **Lovemaking can begin with the glint of an eye; it can go on for hours before either partner slips out of his or her clothes.**

Depending on the moment, quick intense contact can be very satisfying. But sometimes, a steady slow concentration on your partner's expressions or movements, his or her arms or neck or back, can fill you as much as the act of intercourse. Sometimes it can be enough just to kiss for half an hour.

Women's sexual rhythms, as we all know, are vastly different from men's. When the partnership is heterosexual, it is crucial for you to respect your own rhythms; don't let your partner use you for a sperm bank. If he's going too fast, tell him that. Don't let him put his penis inside you until you're ready for him. With practice and desire to give pleasure, your rhythms will blend together. Whether your partner is a man or a woman, it is important that you communicate your needs so that the contact does not leave you hungry.

● Larry Klein, Etc., or Making Sure that You Want to Be Making Love

If you don't want to be touched, say so.

If you want to be touched but don't want to touch, say so.

You're allowed to feel what you feel. And you're allowed to say what you feel. You may not always get what you want, but you are still free to express your feelings and desires.

Don't let yourself, even if it's with someone you love, be talked into making love when you don't want to. You leave yourself open to feelings of resentment and being used; you also leave yourself unsatisfied, and wondering what is wrong, or if you are insatiable.

If your partner gets angry at you when you say no, remember that his or her inability to deal with 'no' is the problem, *not* your sexuality. Chances are that, on hearing no, he or she feels rejected or unloved. Sometimes the problem is communication – being able to remain firm, establish boundaries and care for someone at the same time. And sometimes the problem is that you don't want to be where you are.

Larry Klein had hair like Brillo and beady eyes. He was bossy and mean, but he liked me. He thought I was pretty and that was good enough for me.

I didn't know then that I didn't have to kiss someone just because they wanted to kiss me. Or love someone because they loved me. I was too frightened of never being kissed and never being loved to say no to someone, even with beady eyes and a mean temper, who wanted me.

I'm not frightened anymore. I've learned that kisses, like cold brussel sprouts, don't taste very good when you don't want them.

I don't kiss when I don't want to kiss, just as I don't eat when I don't want to eat. I respect my appetites for food and for sex, and trust that if I say no today, there will always be either kisses or cookies tomorrow.

Spend your hunger for touch the way you spend your hunger for food: on only that, and with only those, who nourish you.

16
On Compulsion

'On a day to day basis, my obsession with food, whether diet food or binge food, is all-consuming. I can't allow myself to feel anything else for anybody else because I'm so obsessed with *me*.'

A Breaking Free workshop participant

'There's so much to see in life; I'm tired of only looking at how fat my thighs are.'

A Breaking Free workshop participant

It was on a Thursday that I returned from my dance class to find a message that Toni, the book publicist, had called. When I reached her she said, *'The Merv Griffin Show* is interested in using you for a spot on their Monday show. At ten o'clock tomorrow morning you have to call the producer for a pre-interview.' Images of Merv Griffin from my childhood floated across my mind: Merv with the dark wavy hair, Merv with the resonant voice.

I'm standing in the kitchen. It's dark outside. I'm hungry. Or am I? *The Merv Griffin Show.* Carob chips, they're in the cupboard. No, the leftover birthday cake. It's frozen, but so what? What do people *wear* on *The Merv Griffin Show*? The first bite of cake melting now in my mouth. What if he asks me about compulsive eating and I get so tongue-tied I wind up telling him about the time Jason and I picked up a couple of hitchhikers and ended up living with them for a year? The third bite of cake is now making its way to my mouth.

'One national show, that's all the book needs,' my editor had said to me a few months before. One national show and what? Do people see me, hear me, and decide they want the book right away?

I look down at what's left of the cake: a pink petal of a flower, half-eaten pieces of yellow cake, dribbles of icing. 'This must be what shooting smack is like,' my friend Tim said about this cake, 'a few minutes gone and you can't think about anything except how fast your body's pumping.'

'That's the whole point, Tim. To stop your feelings. Eat this and your feelings stop because your body starts screaming.' One national show. Everything resting on Merv Griffin.

The movement from anxiety to food is fluid and fast.

Last week, Ariel's ex-lover told her that he was getting married. She came home from work, sat down in a chair, thought about the news, and an hour later she had finished a bottle of wine.

The movement from sadness to alcohol can be fluid and fast.

When I first met Zack he was smoking a joint every day. Six weeks into the relationship he stopped smoking. Six months later he started again. We were in an inn in Mendocino, watching the fire lick the logs. The infatuation part was over. We were down to daily living, two human beings, like two giant puzzles trying to make our pieces fit together. Zack lit up a joint. 'Why are you smoking again?' I asked.

'Because when I first met you it was a whirlwind. Now it's starting to get hard . . . '

The movement from dissatisfaction to drugs can be fluid and fast.

The dictionary defines compulsion as an 'irresistible impulse to perform an irrational act.' Throughout the book, I have contradicted and expanded upon that definition. I have said that there is nothing irrational about a compulsion, that seen in context with the rest of one's life, compulsive behaviour makes perfect sense. A compulsion is a valuable messenger, it tells a story, makes a statement, asks a question, and thereby presents an opportunity to re-examine what has been lost, pushed away, ignored. A compulsion questions the quality of your life; it is an indicator that you are *fighting* for your life. I think that along with such obvious compulsions as alcoholism, drug addiction, cigarette-smoking, and overeating, compulsive behaviour includes relationship-hopping, exercise addiction, continual shopping sprees, workaholism, and spiritual rigidity.

The essence of treating a compulsion is to discover its meaning, to 'decipher' its code as well as to treat it symptomatically according to its physical manifestation.

The first question Merv Griffin asked me was, 'How bad can a compulsion get?' When I began to respond, the woman with whom I was being interviewed, Carol Shaw, the editor of *Big Beautiful Woman* magazine, interrupted and said, 'I want to make it clear that only a small percentage of people who are fat are also compulsive. *Diets* make people compulsive.' Her implication was that when you stop dieting, you stop being compulsive. I agreed that diets precipitate bingeing but not that they make people compulsive.

Pain and the attempt to avoid it make people compulsive. The spectre of the unknown makes people compulsive. Nothing more than the fear of actually revealing and being oneself is what makes people compulsive.

When I binge, for instance, it is usually an indicator that I am unwilling to feel, express, or act on what I'm feeling. The voice of a binge is my own voice turned against myself; it is my voice, which tries and tries to get my attention, tries to speak to me through intuition, my journal, sadness, anger, a feeling in my chest. When I don't listen to that voice, when it realizes that I am ignoring it, it cuts off my connection to it. It cuts me off at the stomach so that I feel clutched and numb and empty. And then it goes haywire.

That voice connects me directly with what is honest in me; it pierces through my fears, my reticence to follow my heart, my anxiety about losing this relationship or that, my concerns about appearance and what people will think. It is the part of me that refuses smiles, kisses, feathery words, docility, or submissiveness when, in a given situation, they would be lies. It speaks what it sees. Sometimes it frightens me. I don't want to know, don't want to listen. And upon seeing that I have ignored it once more, that voice starts talking in the only language it knows will get my attention. Food.

Bingeing is a way of telling myself that something major is going on, that I should slow down and pay attention, and perhaps learn from this one. When I found myself surrounded by frozen cake, I realized that I was feeling tremendous pressure to succeed and it was time, once again, to reiterate for myself what was important to *me* about the book's being published: that it would touch people's lives and provide hope where there had been desperation. Yes, I *wanted* the book to sell. But, if it didn't, if the TV producer didn't like me, if I spoke in non sequiturs to Merv, I needed to remind myself that I could still wake up liking myself. Because for me the book was already a success: The letters and phone calls I'd received were tender and appreciative. If I had eaten until I was sick, taken the eating as an indication of my never-ending obsession with food instead of a signal to remind myself of my priorities, the message behind my eating would have gotten lost, as it did for the seventeen years I spent dieting and bingeing.

I am not saying that we need to be compulsive in order to get through to ourselves, but that when we find ourselves in an activity designed to produce numbness, a voice is present and struggling to be heard.

The value of following that voice is that it takes us to the authentic core of our lives. The difficulty in following that voice is that it takes time and a willingness to pay attention; it presupposes a value on the inner life. Often that voice will not tell us what we think we want to hear. Its message may not be as simple as the need to reiterate one's definition of success. Sometimes – often – what we hear is painful. And we don't know what to do with pain, we don't understand it, aren't taught to value it.

In *Anatomy of an Illness*, Norman Cousins wrote that 'Americans are probably the most pain-conscious people on the face of the earth. For years we have had it drummed into us – in print, on radio, over television, in everyday conversation – that any hint of pain is to be banished as though it were the ultimate evil.'*

At the first sign of pain we take drugs, eat brownies, drink martinis, or work until midnight. At the first sign of pain, we numb ourselves, nauseate ourselves, knock ourselves unconscious. Anything to avoid pain. When a relationship gets difficult, we'd rather switch partners, have an affair, smoke a joint. When we come home night after night exhausted and depleted from our work, we'd rather drink, watch TV, or go to an exercise class than attempt to uncover the source of the problem – which might lead to a re-examination of priorities, beliefs, for-

---

* *Anatomy of an Illness,* Norman Cousins, W.W. Norton & Co., 1979, p. 89.

gotten dreams. We don't expect pain, and when it comes, we want to *do* something with it. We want someone to kiss it and make it better. We want it to go away. In our hearts we are still children waiting for the end of the fairy tale, waiting for it to be *our* turn.

A woman in one of my Breaking Free workshops had lost one hundred pounds on a diet and came to me when she had gained fifty of them back. She said, 'Being thin was a joke. When I wasn't out shopping for sexy new clothes or at a wedding wearing them, I still had to deal with me. Someone, everyone, had lied. The magazines made it look so glorious. Life was supposed to change when I got thin. In a way it did change – my body got smaller and so did my dress size, and I got more attention from men. But in another way, my life *didn't* change. I still had to deal with me. I didn't anymore know how to like myself, how to *be* myself, when I was thin than when I was fat. I wanted to return myself to the manufacturer, get a refund, give up.'

Chubby as a child, not *Vogue* modelish as an adult, this woman grew up thinking that the cause of all her troubles was her excess weight and, conversely, that when she lost that weight, she would be happy. When she discovered that despite being the perfect size, she still felt lonely, got angry, and was easily hurt, she made a decision – albeit an unconscious one – that she would rather have the pain in her life be about her weight, which was in her sole control, than about circumstances, relationships, and emotions that included others and were, therefore, not as controllable. In this way she could continue to translate situations in terms of her weight: If she felt empty inside it was because she was fat; if she felt rejected by a friend or lover it must be that they didn't like her body; if she awoke on a Sunday morning with tears in her eyes it was because she had never stayed thin and was losing out on so much. Not because there might be something missing from her life, something she had promised herself long ago: a story she wanted to write, an instrument she wanted to play, a talk with her great grandmother about growing up in Russia. The pain was not because the grief at her mother's death lay solid like a lump of clay between her breasts, waiting to be recognized and released. No, it was because she wasn't thin. And even though she had gained back fifty of the one hundred pounds, she would lose it again and this time, *this* time would be different, she'd *keep* it off. She could fill her dreamy moments with what she would do, wear, and say when she got thin again, and during the rest of her time she could decide what low-calorie meals she could cook for herself.

And so she could spend the next fifty years of her life this way: gaining weight because she was frightened, then losing it because it would make her happy to do so, then gaining it again because it didn't. She could live this way until she died. And she wouldn't be unusual.

Compulsions are double-edged: They take our focus away from the complex bundle of dreams, wisdom, triumphs, and suffering that is our lives, to a pain that is tangible and ultimately controllable.

None of us lacks for wounds.

I used to think I was unusual: I had taunts at school, troubled parents, people I love died. In a sense I *am* unusual: No one else has lived my life, experienced my joys and pains. But if I am unusual so is my neighbour, so is her daughter. 'Everyone gets abandoned,' my friend Lew once said to me, 'everyone. By a father, mother, a lover. We all have to live through the feeling of having nothing left when people we love walk out, or move away, or die.'

None of us lacks for wounds. Born of imperfect parents, sheathed in bodies that get ill and grow old, we are always subject to the aggressions and torment of others. We all have our stories.

The richness and quality of our lives depends not on pain or the lack of it, but on how we use it. Do we allow its presence, move into its centre, face whatever is crying for attention – or do we try to move faster than the speed of pain, numbing it with food or drink or drugs?

Like the dark side of the moon, our pain is our private face, and in its recognition lies our wholeness and power. Most of us know how to perform in the world. Our personas are glossy and well defined. Our smiles have been perfected, our lines rehearsed. But it is our dark side that holds the promise of renewal and transformation. When we ignore it, its immense power is revealed: Other people become our enemies as we grow alienated from ourselves. What we don't recognize as our own gets projected onto friends, families. Life takes on a bitter edge because we have avoided what could have led us deeper, could have lent purpose and direction to our lives. It is our dark side, unacknowledged, that pushes us to hate, to build bombs, to destroy. In our refusal to face our own shadows, we are left ignorant about the forces that move us. We are stripped of what makes us human: our ability to question what is right, become conscious, move toward the light. In an article in *Yoga Journal*, Helen Caldicott said that ' . . . The leaders of the world . . . don't emotionally know what they are dealing with . . . what these men have to do is get in touch with themselves and find out who they are and why, in fact, they hate. And say, "That is my hatred. I hate because my mother was nasty or my father was cruel. I won't hate the Russians. I won't hate the Jews. I won't hate the blacks. I will own my own anger. And I will love.'"*

The building of bombs and nuclear warheads is a grotesque and horrifying magnification of what happens when we avoid our personal anger, our disappointment, our hatred. We project our shadow outward; we turn the enemy within into countries and continents. We attempt to avoid the pain by developing behaviour that creates numbness to and distance from the source of pain. We anaesthetize ourselves with jargon, ideology, self-righteousness. We forget that the enemy is people – not a point on the map – who laugh and cry and hold each other. Consequently, we never confront the awful pain of killing children, birds, trees – theirs or ours. Our behaviour, like any compulsion, creates a tangible problem that must be dealt with in itself. And this time, with this compulsion, it is the survival of the planet that is threatened.

The beginning is here, with ourselves and our compulsions.

Vulnerability – not sophistication, not intelligence, not power – is what binds us together as humans. We all hunger, fear, hurt, die. When we turn to food, alcohol or drugs, we deny our fragility, confusion and fallibility.

But it's not hopeless.

People change.

They come into a workshop after thirty years of eating when they are in pain, and eating to relieve the pain of eating. However beaten down and ravaged they are, I see a flicker, a force in them stronger than their compulsions, a force that stretches its arms to life, clings and wraps itself around hope like honeysuckle to a vine. If I can show them what I see and if they can use that reflec-

* *Yoga Journal*, June 1982, No. 44, p. 21.

tion to soften their cynicism and to let themselves admit that they still, after so many years, yearn for meaning and love in their lives, the flicker gives way to a flame, the flame to a steady burning fire.

People change; it happens often, constantly. Not only in workshops, but in banks and hospitals, in meeting rooms and living rooms; wherever there is a willingness to be vulnerable, the possibility for change exists.

As a child, I watched *Peter Pan* on television every year. When Tinkerbell, the fairy of light, was dying, the children were asked to clap for her. Clap, children, clap for Tinkerbell. If you want her to live, if you believe in her, then clap for her and your clapping will make her strong.

Every year I cried and clapped and watched the flicker of light get stronger, brighter, until she was well again and shining. I knew that she grew strong because all of us believed that if we clapped as hard as we could, she would brighten. One or two of us weren't enough; it took of all of us, everywhere.

Clap hard. Clap strong. Because everywhere you look, there is a flickering – and everytime you clap, it gets stronger.

17
Conclusion:
Through Thick and Thin

'Life is so much better for me now. I have cried
more in the last year than I have in the last ten
years. I'm willing to sit and look inside to find
out what is going on with me. I'm willing to be
in pain (most of the time) when it occurs. I'm
willing to feel what I feel. I'm much more able
to ask for what I want and much more willing
to say what I feel to others. I eat what I want
when I want and it is wonderful. I enjoy food so
much now and I get pleasure from it. I also
allow more pleasure in my life in other ways. I
can join someone for dinner and tell them I'm
not hungry. I can refuse to eat a "special treat"
someone has made if I don't feel like eating it.
I feel as if years of old, stuffed-down feelings
are pouring out of me. I feel as if I'm cleaning
myself and beginning anew. It is an ongoing
process which will never stop.'

A Breaking Free workshop participant

Agatha, my assistant, told me that when her seven-
year-old son learned about infinity, he came to her and
said, 'Tell me, Mummy, tell me that there is an end.'

There is.

And there isn't.

There is no end to the self-flagellation, the punishment, the doubt and the anguish of compulsive eating.
There is an end to the torturous way you interpret what
you do with food, an end to using your eating against
yourself. There is an end to classifying actions as good or
bad or right or wrong and to classifying food as 'permis-

sible' and 'not permissible.' There is an end to defining overeating as failure. There is an end to the half-crazed feeling of never-ending hunger. There is an end to wanting it to end.

There isn't an end to eating every day or to making mistakes. There isn't an end to fluctuations in weight. There isn't an end to change. There is no such thing as arriving and never having to work with yourself again.

There isn't an end to feeling increasingly connected to and compassionate with yourself and those around you.

There isn't an end to the joy of forever growing.

Index

Cookery handbooks now available in Panther Books

L D Michaels
The Complete Book of Pressure Cooking   £1.95 □

Cecilia Norman
Pancakes & Pizzas   95p □
Microwave Cookery Course   £1.95 □
The Pie and Pastry Cookbook   £2.50 □
Barbecue Cookery   £1.50 □

Franny Singer
The Slow Crock Cookbook   £1.95 □

Janet Walker
Vegetarian Cookery   £1.50 □

Pamela Westland
Bean Feast   £1.95 □
The Complete Grill Cookbook   £1.50 □
High-Fibre Vegetarian Cookery   £1.95 □

Marika Hanbury Tenison
Deep-Freeze Cookery   £1.95 □
Cooking with Vegetables   £1.95 □

Sheila Howarth
Grow, Freeze and Cook   £1.50 □

Jennifer Stone
The Alcoholic Cookbook   £1.25 □

Beryl Wood
Let's Preserve It   £1.50 □

Barbara Griggs
Baby's Cookbook   £1.95 □

Wendy Craig
Busy Mum's Cookbook   £1.95 □

Carolyn Heal and Michael Allsop
Cooking with Spices   £2.95 □

To order direct from the publisher just tick the titles you want
and fill in the order form.   HB681

Health and self-help books now available in Panther Books

W H Bates
Better Eyesight Without Glasses £1.95 ☐

Ronald Gatty
The Body Clock Diet £1.50 ☐

Desmonde Dunne
Yoga Made Easy £1.95 ☐

Laurence E Morehouse & Leonard Gross
Total Fitness £1.95 ☐
Maximum Performance £1.50 ☐

Constance Mellor
Guide to Natural Health £1.25 ☐
Natural Remedies for Common Ailments £1.95 ☐

Sonya Richmond
Yoga and Your Health £1.25 ☐

Phyllis Speight
Homoeopathy £1.50 ☐

Kenneth Lysons
How to Cope with Hearing Loss 95p ☐

Dr Richard B Stuart
Act Thin, Stay Thin £1.50 ☐

Dr Carl C Pfeiffer & Jane Banks
Total Nutrition £1.50 ☐

Dr Hamilton Hall
Be Your Own Back Doctor £1.95 ☐

José Silva and Michael Miele
The Silva Mind Control Method £2.50 ☐

Dr Peter M Miller
The Change Your Metabolism Diet £1.95 ☐

Slimming Magazine
30-Day Formula £3.95 ☐

To order direct from the publisher just tick the titles you want and fill in the order form.

HB881

All these books are available at your local bookshop or newsagent, or can be ordered direct from the publisher.

To order direct from the publisher just tick the titles you want and fill in the form below.

Name_____

Address _____

_____

Send to:
Panther Cash Sales
PO Box 11, Falmouth, Cornwall TR10 9EN.

Please enclose remittance to the value of the cover price plus:

UK 45p for the first book, 20p for the second book plus 14p per copy for each additional book ordered to a maximum charge of £1.63.

BFPO and Eire 45p for the first book, 20p for the second book plus 14p per copy for the next 7 books, thereafter 8p per book.

Overseas 75p for the first book and 21p for each additional book.